PRAEGER WORLD OF ART SERIES

A Concise History of
IRISH ART

A Concise History of
IRISH ART

Bruce Arnold

FREDERICK A. PRAEGER, Publishers
NEW YORK · WASHINGTON

BOOKS THAT MATTER

PUBLISHED IN THE UNITED STATES OF AMERICA IN
1968 BY FREDERICK A. PRAEGER, INC., PUBLISHERS
III FOURTH AVENUE, NEW YORK, N.Y. 10003

© 1968, IN LONDON, ENGLAND, BY BRUCE ARNOLD

LIBRARY OF CONGRESS CATALOG CARD NUMBER:
68-54497

PRINTED IN GREAT BRITAIN

Contents

Introduction

There is a widely held fallacy that Ireland's contribution to the art of the world has been almost exclusively in the realm of the written word. This book is an attempt to prove otherwise. For example, it is difficult to say which of the two Yeats brothers was the greater artist, Jack the painter, or William the poet. The question is answerable in more than just personal terms. The fine early drawings repeatedly strike echoes in the lyrics of the rhymer. And a great poem like 'Sailing to Byzantium' can almost be taken as a direct comment on the shadowy world of a great painting like *About to Write a Letter*. In the painting   *Ill. 1* the vision of the artist has become universal and immensely powerful. And in the poem the same thing has happened. The two can strike chords in each other, and it is even possible to imagine the pensive, hesitant figure in oil paint speaking the lines–

> *Consume my heart away; sick with desire*
> *And fastened to a dying animal*
> *It knows not what it is; and gather me*
> *Into the artifice of eternity.*

Yeats the poet was a figure to be reckoned with at the turn of the century. He was a legend in his own lifetime, and while his brother was still only understood and loved by a small group of admirers, the poet was regarded as one of the great writers of the twentieth century. There has been some change in this state of affairs during the last ten or fifteen years, yet still Jack B. Yeats remains an under-rated and unexplored artist, and, what is more important from the point of view of this book, he is to a great extent regarded as a unique and un-

7

characteristic phenomenon in a country which has little or no tradition of visual art, and no artists in the past of comparable stature.

The visual arts in Ireland during the early Christian period are well-known and justly celebrated. What is not accepted to

I JACK B. YEATS
About to Write a Letter

anything like the same extent is the fact that various artistic
traditions were established during the intervening centuries
since the golden ages in which the Book of Kells, the Ardagh   *Ills 21–3*
Chalice and the Cross of Cong were produced, and that these   *14, 31–2*
traditions grew, expanded and enriched themselves, and

9

ultimately produced artists of considerable stature. Various forces, however, have operated against the emergence of any clear idea of Irish art, with a character and style of its own. History has given to most of the artists of the seventeenth, eighteenth and nineteenth centuries the unfortunate labels of 'Anglo-Irish', 'Ascendancy' or 'Plantation'. Many of the better Irish artists have been forced by circumstance, or persuaded by ambition, to seek a better fortune in London, and their reclamation here may seem impertinent. Still others are known by a mere handful of paintings, the majority of their work having been re-attributed, and their pictures now masquerading in public collections under more illustrious names.

In spite of the temptations to be greedy about individual artists in pinning Irish nationality upon them, my first concern has been with the idea of an Irish art, developing, changing and enriching itself in spite of history rather than because of it. Artists tend to be the least patriotic of men, and the question of nationalism is not one with which they are greatly concerned. Yet in many areas – landscape, topography, portraiture, historical painting, silver, glass, even architecture – a distinctive national style and character, a difference of light, a sense of history evolving and of people being involved in it, are all contributory factors to the overall idea which has been the mainspring of this book.

In a number of areas it covers ground which has not been touched on before. While the art of early Christian Ireland has been extensively studied by Mlle Françoise Henry and other scholars, there is no general history covering either the period since then or any considerable section of it. Invaluable work has been done on individual artists, notably by W. G. Strickland in his *Dictionary of Irish Artists* and by Thomas Bodkin, but their works are hard to come by, and, in the case of the former, tend to be rather academic in appeal. Much of the other published material is listed in the Bibliography.

I would like to thank the many people who gave me help and advice in the writing of this book.

The Celtic era

Irish art begins as abstract art: the ritual decoration by early Bronze Age man of the tombs of his ancestors. His art is a complex pattern of loops and spirals, diamonds, zig-zags, triangles and squares, pecked out in the granite kerb-stones, and cut into the pillars and stone slabs of passage graves and burial chambers. The artist-sculptor follows the shape and contour of the stone on which he works. His thinking is three-dimensional, and his concern is with harmony, rhythm and the balanced pattern of simple abstract forms, rather than with any attempt at representational art reflecting his immediate animal or vegetable environment. In this sense it seems spiritual in nature, belonging to the realms of pagan magic, possibly part of a heathen religious cult which in all other respects is lost to us for ever.

It begins a tradition in art that can be traced from the early Bronze Age to the first full flowering of Irish art in the immensely rich early Christian Celtic period, from the coming of Saint Patrick to the war and desolation of the Viking invasion of the ninth century.

In its early, pre-Christian period it should not be seen as a national art. Ireland was part of the Celtic world, and her art closely tied up with Celtic culture, a European phenomenon, stretching from Spain to the Scandinavian countries, and from Hungary to the Atlantic coasts of Kerry and Donegal. The Celtic world knew no centre, nor was it conscious of its own unity. Its peoples were far-flung and communication between them was immensely difficult and slow. Yet in language, myth, ritual, belief, literature and art they were one. And when Diodorus, in the first century B C, was describing the Celts of Gaul in his history of the world, he was really speaking of one people whose territories had covered most of Europe and whose racial characteristics were identical far beyond the confines of the area he was writing about. What he had to say about the Celtic people and their distinctive character tells us much about their art:

> In conversation they use few words and speak in riddles, for the most part hinting at things and leaving a great deal to be understood. They frequently exaggerate with the aim of extolling themselves and diminishing the status of others. They are boasters and threateners and given to bombastic self-dramatization, and yet they are quick of mind and with good natural ability for learning.

It is not surprising that such a people, with so distinctive an attitude to the unconquered world they lived in, so different from the Romans or the Vikings, their latter-day vanquishers, should have produced an art of such originality, refinement and style.

The earliest manifestations are of uncertain date. The great heathen sanctuary at New Grange, in County Meath, may be as early as 3000 B C. The passage grave at Knowth, which resembles it in many respects, has been dated approximately at 2500 B C. And the graves at Carrow Keel belong to the same

2 The decorated kerb-stone at the entrance to the burial chamber at New Grange, Co. Meath, *c.* 3000 B C

period. Yet Iron Age remains have been found at the last of these, and it is reasonable to suspect that these tombs and sanctuaries, dating originally from the Neolithic period, passed down through the centuries into the Bronze Age and the Iron Age, without losing their sacred significance. What is fairly certain is that the decorations we have from these tombs belong as firmly to Celtic art as do the decorated pages in the Lindisfarne Gospels, or the carved panels on the Cross of Moone.

Ill. 18
Ills 26–7
Ill. 2

The kerb-stone at New Grange is covered in a close pattern of spirals, the most common of all the motifs decorating these tombs, and one basic to all Celtic art. The lines flow into one another, the shapes adapt themselves to the contour of the stone; at one point the spirals give way to a diamond pattern, breaking the subtle harmony and introducing a note of paradox at the end of this silent motto.

Other decorations at New Grange and Knowth vary considerably from this one. There are even primitive attempts at representational art, including the strangely distorted figure of an animal. But in general these early beginnings establish form and pattern and abstract balance as the basis, and it was to continue so, even after animals, birds, plants and human forms had superseded the simple geometric patterns of this early period.

Ill. 3   The Bronze Age is rich in gold ornaments. Again the dating of these must remain speculative, but many have been placed with reasonable certainty at different periods of the time-span from 2000 BC down to the late Iron Age, and the finds in Ireland have been rich enough to give a quite clear idea of the developments in style and decoration from the early and very simple torcs and lunulae to the complex design and craftsman-

Ill. 6   ship of the Broighter Collar dating from the first century AD, and showing, in its elliptical curves and spirals and the depth of the relief work, close relationship with the style of La Tène,

Ill. 4   the late Iron Age Celtic era, regarded by many as the true fountain-head of Celtic art. The earliest of these ornaments are very simple. The gold is plain, sometimes twisted into a spiral, and the catch to fasten these early torcs round the neck is nothing more than two lumps of gold at the ends which shoulder into one another. It is only much later that such

14

elaborate clasps as the one on the collar which adorns the Roman marble effigy of *The Dying Gaul*, close in style to the Broighter Collar, were introduced. Restrained decoration in the form of geometric patterns, particularly around the borders and at the tips of the lunulae and on other ornaments, including the gold discs found in various places in Ireland, first appear around 1800 BC. There is not enough material to show us quite how the elaboration of craftsmanship and design progressed, but a thousand years later, at the beginning of the Iron Age, the same basic collar design has changed radically. The crafts- *Ill. 5* manship of the Glenisheen Gorget is of a high order. The points have been replaced by discs, profusely patterned with smaller circles in a strictly geometric design, and the lines and zig-zags cut into the surfaces of the earlier collars have given way to plain carefully ridged curves, alternating with gadrooned rims of a very high quality.

3 Gold hoard, inclu-ding necklets and brace-lets, Bronze Age

4 Celtic gold torc, late Iron Age

Ill. 5   The Gleninsheen Gorget does not, however, display any of
the highly distinctive design associated with La Tène and
Ill. 6   apparent in the Broighter Collar, and it is reasonable to assume
that the most significant Celtic wave of all arrived in Ireland at
a later period during the Iron Age, possibly as a result of the
Gallic Wars and the growing pressures of Roman civilization.
Ill. 7   The Turoe Stone in County Galway shows close affinities in
its spiral and elliptical decorations with the designs on the

5 The Gleninsheen Gor-
get, eighth century BC

6 The Broighter Collar,
from the Broighter gold
hoard, first century AD

7 The Turoe Stone
(Co. Galway),
La Tène period

16

Broighter Collar, and, in all probability, belongs to the La Tène *Ill. 6* period. It is quite small, less than five feet high, and its true purpose is unknown, though it was probably a religious cult object. What is interesting is that the sculptor who decorated it maintained his distinctive style of ornamentation with a well-developed sense of balance and form and a considerable awareness of the three-dimensional effect he wished finally to achieve.

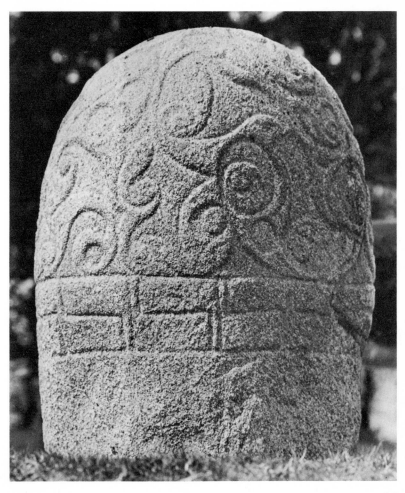

Art in Ireland during the pagan period remains a rich but very puzzling heritage. Its beginnings are obscure, and without the sharp interruption of a Roman invasion, so pervasive an influence in Britain, and with the limited evidence at our disposal, even the later centuries which ushered in the Christian era with the coming of Saint Patrick, are shrouded in relative obscurity.

Christianity brought to Ireland in the fifth century conditions under which art could develop and flourish. It brought a central and most powerful belief round which the many and diverse facets of pagan art could be unified and re-directed, and the peaceful nature of the conversion of Ireland did nothing to alienate the highly developed Celtic society and culture, which in its Christian form was to survive for another five hundred years. To begin with, the monastic settlements were humble and primitive in the extreme. But they flourished on the merits of their teaching, and they grew and spread rapidly through the land until king and bishop stood side by side. The new medieval duality of church and state became an established part of the Irish social framework.

While it is not possible to deal in detail with the structure of Irish society at this time, certain aspects of it need to be understood if the art produced by the country is to be seen in its true perspective. Celtic society was rural and tribal. There were no cities and no walled towns. The territorial unit was a small one, and was ruled by a king who might also have supremacy over the kings of neighbouring tribes, although this would not give him sovereignty over the people of such tribes. Eventually this structure led to the highest class of king known to the laws: the king of a province. The idea of a single king of Ireland is a relatively late one. It was probably first claimed by Niall of the Nine Hostages as late as the fifth century, during the first quarter of which he reigned. The claim to an Irish monarchy was certainly perpetuated by his descendants for six centuries afterwards, but theirs was quite often a theoretical rather than an actual supremacy.

Within each kingdom – and there were many, and they were small – there existed a quite strict hierarchy upon which many aspects of the law were based. At its top stood the king, tracing his right to kingship back through many generations to one or other of the ancestral deities. Next to him were the various degrees of nobility, the aristocracy or warrior class, those whose family trees were preserved among the genealogies and those of gentle birth. Whether there was much variation among the nobility beyond the natural one of wealth is open to question. Between them and the commoners there was a special, professional class of men whose skills gave them a status beyond the one to which they were born. They were called *aes dana* – 'men of art' – and as well as poets, historians, musicians, lawyers and other skilled or highly trained men, they included those responsible for the early works of art discussed in this history. They form the most interesting of the social orders in early Irish society, and while they are placed between the nobility and the commoner, they are much closer to the former, with a powerful voice and an influential position.

Another aspect of this early Irish society, and an important one where the laws of the land were concerned, was the fact that the unit of society was not the individual, but the kin. The smallest kin-group recognized by society was a four-generation group. This was the normal property-owning unit, and it was as a group responsible for the liabilities of its members. The law was concerned with inter-group matters rather than with the internal affairs of kindred.

Such a society does not construct for itself the kind of institutions which were introduced into Britain as a result of the Roman invasion. To take one basic example: early Irish society had no need for efficient roads. Throughout the country the tribal system was a closely interwoven one: but it knew no centre, and required no general communications system. There were no cities to go to. Trade was effected by barter. Kingdoms were independent of each other, or where they were interdependent the balance was a fairly equal one.

But if much of the sophisticated development of the intricate structure of a nation or a state in the modern sense of the word was not undertaken by early Irish society, there was no reason why such a society should not be capable of producing great art and literature. The privileged position enjoyed by the artist and craftsman would have been envied by his equivalent in Europe during the eighteenth century. The system of patronage, together with the privileges accorded to ability, both technical and intellectual, did in fact produce works of art and literature of the highest order.

The coming of Christianity in the fifth century did not alter this social structure to any profound degree. If anything, the beliefs were absorbed by the society and adapted to their own needs. Certainly, within the four centuries between the beginning of the Christian mission to Ireland and the coming of the Vikings, much of the known fabric of society in the country remained surprisingly unchanged, and it was short-term Viking militance rather than four centuries of Christian influence from Rome that imposed upon the country so elementary a thing as the idea of a city.

No clear picture is possible. Much of what is said about Irish society at this time is highly speculative. Where the Celtic world is concerned scholarship still stands very much on the threshold, and in many respects this will always remain so. The works of art which have come down to us are themselves enigmatic. We know their quality; in most cases we know their function; and we know certain aspects of the society which produced them. But the contact we achieve through them with the society which produced them is often broken by fundamental and far-reaching gaps in our knowledge and understanding.

Although the conversion of Ireland began in the fifth century, it is not really until the middle of the seventh century that the astonishing sequence of masterpieces of early Christian Celtic art in Ireland commenced. Nevertheless the period from AD 432 up to the first years of the seventh century produced important and distinctive prototypes for the later flowering.

They include many bronze objects, some with enamel work, the earliest engraved stone slabs, and the 'Cathach', a copy of the Psalms preserved in the Royal Irish Academy, and traditionally ascribed to Saint Columba.

Perhaps the most famous and most elaborate of these early metal objects is the 'Petrie Crown', a bronze tomb decoration. *Ill. 8* The relief work in the metal is open and assured. The design, made up of elliptical curves and scrolls, is well balanced; and while the highly stylized head of a beast is used as part of the design, the overall effect is abstract and austerely simple. Some of the earlier penannular brooches belong to this period, and most of them show Roman influence in the design. But while the indirect influence of the Roman empire, which had so changed the society across the Irish Sea, made itself felt in various ways, Ireland was also open to, and received, artistic impulses from many other sources including Egypt, Syria, Greece, Armenia, perhaps even Persia.

8 The 'Petrie Crown', bronze tomb decoration

The earliest stone sculpture follows the pagan style of decoration without any attempt to shape the stone. Flat engraved slabs bear simple designs of the cross, often within a circle, and with various extensions of the design around or underneath. Only at the end of the sixth century does the cross actually emerge from the slab as a carved shape, one of the earliest examples of this being the crude but vigorous Carn-

Ill. 9 donagh Cross in Donegal. This monument, while its outline is unrefined, has a fascinating wealth of carving on it, from the intricate interweavings which cover the top, the animals and birds which lurk in corners of the design, to the round-faced, simple but pious figure standing beneath with arms outstretched in a universal benediction.

With the seventh century technical perfection and a stylistic independence brought about a synthesis in the art of metalwork, sculpture and manuscript illumination, and a sequence of Celtic masterpieces in each of these spheres began.

One of the earliest and finest of the illuminated manuscripts
Ills 10–12 is the Book of Durrow. It is a copy of the Gospels, and came originally from the monastery founded in Durrow, County Offaly, by Saint Columba. It was for a time in the possession of a farmer who used to dip it in the drinking water used by his cattle as a cure for disease. It passed eventually into the hands of the Cromwellian Bishop of Meath who presented it to the Trinity College Library.

The book is smaller in page size than most of the other Irish illuminated manuscripts, and employs a relatively limited range of colours in the decoration – strong red, bright yellow and dark green. The outlines to the drawings and the backgrounds to the interlacings are in dark brown, probably black when first done. The text, which is the Latin Vulgate, is done in Irish majuscule, and the initial letter and opening lines of Saint Mark's Gospel display certain distinctive characteristics of the Book of Durrow. One is the use of dots to give a field of colour without making the effect too solid. Dots are also used to emphasize outline, as in the smaller initial letters, and to add

22

9 The Carndonagh Cross (Co. Donegal), late sixth century

colour without too much boldness to the main decoration.

Ill. 10 The initial N is abstract in design, relying primarily on panels of interweaving and spirals. The abstract nature of the design is maintained throughout the book. Only rarely, as at the beginning of the Gospel of Saint John, do the involved interlacings turn from abstract ribbons of colour into elongated and strangely contorted beasts, their jaws locked into their own or another's flesh, their bodies woven into patterns of ordered distortion and subtle balance which stand out with an almost fierce intensity of colour from the dark background.

But the finest pages of all are those depicting the symbols of the four Apostles. In them the artist has displayed immense

10 Book of Durrow, Initial page of Saint Mark's Gospel, seventh century

11 Book of Durrow, Evangelist's symbol of Saint Mark, seventh century

12 Book of Durrow, Saint Matthew, seventh century

range of understanding of the value of contrast, the use of white space, the modulation of colour by using dots and lines, and the considerable potential of his limited palette. In the symbol page for Saint Mark's Gospel the highly stylized and ferocious *Ill. 11* lion stands in profile, his body outlined in yellow and covered in a pattern of red and green diamonds, his head, with its staring yellow eye, a far from haphazard carpet of red dots which emphasize the formal and stylized nature of the drawing and modify the contrast between the beast and its background of plain cream-coloured vellum. The simple border to the page is made up of four panels of interlacings, the side ones narrow and involved, but made light in overall effect by the use of dots,

25

the top and bottom panels much stronger, with solid colouring, more dark brown background visible and a design of greater simplicity and boldness which holds the page together.

The book is difficult to date, and some aspects of it have long been the subject of academic controversy. There are Saxon influences in the design, there are visual relationships with decorations on the Carndonagh Cross, the Tara Brooch and the Ardagh Chalice, and the relationship with Lindisfarne, from which another of the great illuminated manuscripts of the period originated, is explained by the fact that both monasteries were Columban. While it is highly accomplished in its craftsmanship and technique, the artistic conception is comparatively simple and experimental in both colour and design. There are none of the sophisticated flights of the imagination which characterize such manuscripts as the Book of Kells, and in this lies much of the strength and delight of the earlier work.

The best qualities of the Book of Durrow, the restraint, the balance, the formal dignity, the exuberant but disciplined imagination, are epitomized in the finest example of Irish metalwork of the early Christian period, the Ardagh Chalice. Mlle Françoise Henry, in her *Irish Art in the Early Christian Period*, says 'the whole balance of the composition has still the strength and restraint of the best seventh-century work and belongs to that moment of perfection that marks the turning point between a youthful, impetuous, though already experienced art, and a surfeited and over-elaborate decoration.' The parallel between the two works is quite close. Much of the surface area of silver is quite plain, and this serves to emphasize the richness, brilliance and intricacy of the panels of gold filigree and the red and blue glass studs which cluster below the handles and divide up the panels of decoration. The chalice has a plain rim, reinforced with brass. Below it there is a broad band divided by glass studs into ten panels, all of which are decorated in the most delicate and complex gold filigree work. The design of each of the studs is based on the cross. The names of the Apostles are lightly engraved in the silver below this band

26

of gold panelling, and then in the centre of each side is another cross, simple in its basic design, but richly decorated, again with glass studs and gold filigree work, and employing fairly simple spiral patterns. The bowl of the chalice is joined to its base by a thick bronze stem, heavily gilt, and worked in the most intricate and involved of all the decorations on the cup. The other concentration of rich colour and pattern occurs at each of the handles. These are decorated with coloured glass panels in red, blue, green and yellow interspersed with tiny frames of gold filigree work of great craftsmanship and complexity. The concentrations of gold and glass are outlined on the plain surface of the silver with lines and dots, and the panels and particularly the studs of glass are heavily embossed, the main ones standing out more than half an inch from the surface of the silver bowl. In the originality of its overall conception, in the working of the silver and gold, in the manipulation of moulded, coloured glass, in the simple, light engraved work on the silvery-grey metal, the Ardagh Chalice stands out as a supreme *Ill. 14* example of early Irish art at its best. And it was found just one hundred years ago by a young boy who was digging in a field of potatoes at Ardagh, County Limerick. With it was a smaller bronze chalice and four penannular brooches, all of them now in the National Museum, Dublin.

The form of these penannular brooches, while they have always been regarded as peculiarly Irish, and have acted as a somewhat baleful influence on jewellery and design down to the present day, derives from a design that is basically Roman. There are numerous examples, varying considerably in style and in workmanship. They have no specifically Christian significance, and are as likely to have formed part of the personal adornment of kings or queens as of bishops of the church. The finest of them all, the Tara Brooch, is unusually close in style *Ill. 13* to the Ardagh Chalice. It has no connection with Tara, the seat of the High Kings of Ireland, and was in fact found in a wooden box near the mouth of the River Boyne, along with other objects, in all probability abandoned loot. It is one of the

13 The Tara Brooch, early eighth century

smallest of these brooches, and certainly the finest and richest *Ill. 13* example of Celtic jewellery to come down to us. It consists of a closed ring in cast silver with an ornamental pin attached by a loose ring; there is a silver mesh chain attached to one side, and it is assumed that the brooch is one of a pair, originally joined together across the shoulders. Both the front and the back are decorated. The casting of the front is in the form of deep open panels into which gold filigree work, close in style to the work on the Ardagh Chalice, was inset. A number of these panels are *Ill. 14* now empty, but the remaining examples reveal a remarkable delicacy and fineness of work, and a highly original inspiration. Beasts with pronounced eyes and lips curl and intertwine in raised threads of gold within spaces that at times are no more

14 The Ardagh Chalice, early eighth century

than quarter of an inch square; and the abstract decoration has an inexhaustible variety. At key points in the design there are glass and amber studs, some of them crowned with filigree work and gold granulation. Copper has been used in the larger

Ill. 13 panels, and it adds to the range of colour produced by the gold and the silver. The back of the brooch lacks the depth and relief effect of the front, but is equally rich in design, and is even closer in the style of the glass studding to the same decorative

Ill. 14 feature on the Ardagh Chalice. It belongs to the same period, and may conceivably have come from the same workshop, even from the hand of the same anonymous craftsman. Certainly the outstanding quality of brooch and chalice which raises them so firmly above other similar discoveries also draws them closer together, and that is as much as one is able to say with any certainty.

There are other important examples of monastic art from

Ill. 15 this period. The origins of the Saint John's Crucifixion Plaque are probably quite different from those of the brooch and chalice. It is one of the earliest representations in Irish art of the Crucifixion, and dates from the late seventh century. The central figure of Christ with arms outstretched and nailed to

Ill. 9 the shaped cross resembles the figure on the Carndonagh Cross in Donegal, but much of the decoration, which includes a herring-bone pattern, unusual spirals and zig-zags and combinations of cross and circle, are not to be found elsewhere. The plaque may have decorated a shrine or a book cover. The Moylough Belt Reliquary, a bronze shrine for a leather belt, probably that of a saint, is fairly close in style to the chalice, and rich in bird and animal representation done in the form of buckles and fasteners around the shrine. Less ornate but contemporary bells, brooches, altar vessels, reliquaries, bronze mounts and other early Christian examples of art survive, and their discovery throughout the country, coupled with their distinctive and homogeneous style, point to a richly organic tradition of which we are, today, the inheritors of only a tiny portion.

30

15 Saint John's Crucifixion Plaque, late seventh century

To understand the development of Irish art from the eighth century on, the expansion of Irish missionary activity into Scotland and England must be appreciated. Whereas the early art displays a remarkable unity of design and inspiration, the later art of the eighth and ninth centuries is modified in its styles and trends by the fact that monastic artists were working further and further away from their aesthetic roots, and were more and more open to influences within the countries they sought to convert, or to which they came with the offer of their sophisticated but highly individual skills. This is most effectively demonstrated in terms of Irish illuminated manuscripts. They are the most portable of relics, which is itself something of a disadvantage when it comes to tracing origin, but at the same time they are richly distinctive in style, impart considerable information through linguistics, calligraphy and their colophons, and have been the object of careful preservation – with notable exceptions – for a far longer period of time than has the

Ills 10–12 sculpture, the metalwork or the jewellery. Just as nothing equals in its own sphere the powerful simplicity of the Book of Durrow, so nothing equals the richly complex and diverse

Ills 21–3 range of the Book of Kells, written and illuminated little more than a century later. And between the two may be placed with reasonable assurance a wealth of illuminated Gospels and other devotional books, all of them derived from Irish artists, and

Ill. 20 including the Books of Dimma, Armagh, Mulling, Mac Regol, Saint Chad (also known as the Lichfield Gospels), the Lindisfarne Gospels, the Stowe Missal, the Saint Gall and the

Ill. 16 Echternach manuscripts.

Ill. 17 The Book of Saint Chad, preserved now in Lichfield Cathedral, is an example of the 'wandering' manuscript. Its place of origin is not known, and the earliest mention of its movements is contained in some notes in Welsh on the manuscript itself, recording that it was exchanged for a horse, and subsequently given to Saint Teliau and placed in the monastery of Llandaff, near the Bristol Channel. This was at the end of the eighth century, up to a hundred years after the writing of the

32

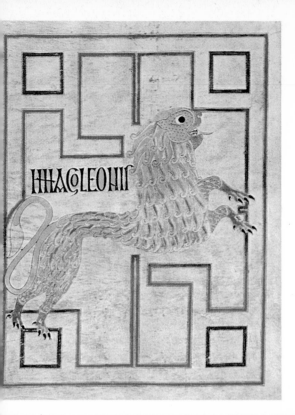

16 Echternach Gospels,
symbol of Saint Mark, *c.* 690

17 Lichfield Gospels, two symbols
of the Evangelists, seventh century

manuscript. It passed to Lichfield Cathedral two centuries later, and is still in the library there. It is incomplete and much damaged, particularly the colouring. But what is left to us still provides a considerable variety of styles, and qualities of drawing and design. They range from the relatively simple portrait pages of the four Apostles to the high sophistication of the ornamental page with its multitudes of birds and animals, their contortions carried to extremes, their overall effect florid *Ill. 17* and obtuse, but strangely satisfying and in concept remarkably original. There is almost an element of optical illusion in the way the outline of the cross emerges from the mass of scrolls, twists and curves, and then is lost again, only to re-emerge as the eye continues its voyage of discovery among the innumerable, tangled beasts.

While it is possible that the Book of Saint Chad at Lichfield was done in Ireland, it is almost certain that the Lindisfarne *Ills 18–19* Gospels, which are quite close in style and treatment, were written and illuminated by Eadfrith, Bishop of Lindisfarne from 698 to 721. Irish monks had taught at Lindisfarne for some considerable time, and Eadfrith himself had spent six years studying in Ireland at the end of the seventh century, so that the closeness of this work to the tradition of Irish art is not really in dispute. The manuscript, which is in an excellent state of preservation, is in the British Museum. The range of colours used in the illustrations is extensive, with several shades of the principal blue, red and yellow. Influences on the style of the artist have broadened, and Mediterranean traits of a Greek or Byzantine origin are present, particularly in the portraits of the Apostles. But the Book of Lindisfarne is still essentially Irish, its decoration and its lettering revealing an amalgam of characteristics from various sources, much of the perverse *Ill. 17* animal decoration coming from the Book of Saint Chad, while the simpler devices, the interlacings, the dots and the spirals *Ills 10–12* show direct descent from the Book of Durrow. Françoise *Ills 18–19* Henry says of the Lindisfarne Gospels, 'The whole decoration is permeated by a sort of frozen perfection,' and in spite of its

34

18 Lindisfarne Gospels, The Chi-Rho, late seventh century

pristine condition and its aesthetic completeness and unity, one is inclined to agree. It is the work of a very gifted pupil of Irish teachers whose academic understanding is extensive, but whose deeper sympathies with the origins of the Celtic tradition in which he works are absent.

As well as the large illuminated manuscripts, usually designed to rest on the altars, there are a number of much smaller books, with abbreviated texts, possibly made light so that they could be carried easily by bands of monks setting out on pilgrimages, or on missions to other kingdoms. One of the finest of these

35

is the Book of Dimma in the Trinity College Library in Dublin. *Ill. 20*
It is somewhat cruder in style than the larger books, but colourful
and vigorous. It is the work of more than one scribe, and was
written at the monastery in Roscrea, County Tipperary,
probably towards the middle of the eighth century. In the
planning of the illuminated pages, in its colour range, in the
interlacings and the use of dots, it displays all the simpler
strengths which makes the Book of Durrow so fine an example *Ills 10–12*
of the art of this early period.

19 Lindisfarne Gospel, 'Carpet
Page', late seventh century

20 Book of Dimma, symbol
of Saint John, seventh century

Three other small decorated manuscripts belong to the same period: the Stowe Manuscript in the Library of the Royal Irish Academy, the Book of Mulling, and a much restored but finely drawn Gospel fragment in the British Museum.

Ills 21–3 The supreme achievement of Irish Celtic art, however, is the Book of Kells, which probably dates from the second half of the eighth century. In it all the diverse strands and developments in Irish art seem to reach perfect fruition. It is strong and original in its design. Its range of colours and their use are intensely sophisticated. Its script is beautifully clear and rounded, and the decorations run through it, their wild and varied flights of imagination bringing colour and invention to the opening letters of sentences throughout the pages of text. Sometimes these decorations in the script assume the proportion of major illuminations, as in the treatment of the Beatitudes, in Saint Matthew's Gospel, where the whole length of the page is decorated with eight capital Bs, each of them formed out of serpent bodies, four with human heads, four with the heads of birds, all richly coloured in turquoise, violet and golden brown. At other times these decorations are small, obscure, and often surprisingly comic representations of insects, animals, birds and human figures, peering from behind letters, lurking in the corners of pages, floating between the lines or in the margins. Sometimes the figure of an angel or an Apostle peers over the top of one of the initial letters or decorative panels, and his feet jut out beneath. And yet these decorations do not impinge on the clear bold script, which runs on with smooth precision through the 339 leaves of the book which have survived. Only in the great illuminated pages is the emphasis reversed. In these portraits, Gospel scenes, full pages of ornament and introductory pages of decoration, the artist takes over with his balanced mixture of invention and discipline. His range of colours is considerable. It includes the frequent use of different shades of mauve, several shades of yellow, blue, brown, green and red. His sense of space and balance on the page is excellent, and the range of design and symbol embodies all the discoveries

38

of the earlier artists known to us from other books from Irish monasteries. But there is something more which raises the Book of Kells to its pre-eminent position, something that makes *Ills 21–3* of it a perfect work of art in spite of conflicting styles, unfinished pages and uneven quality. It is not easily defined, but is perhaps best explained by the fact that the central element in the wide range of decoration and ornament in the Book of Kells is Man. The earlier abstract designs, the spirals, the interlacings, the woven patterns and the dots are there; the later foliage, and the richly diverse Celtic bestiary are also there; but instead of being central, as in the many manuscripts so far considered, they now all revolve around the figure of Man. Man is presented as Christ, as Angel, as Apostle, as Devil, or as mere onlooker in a scene, such as the Temptation of Christ or His *Ill. 23* arrest in the Garden of Gethsemane; but the essential human involvement, leading to the full response of emotion and intellect, which is and must be part of any great work of art, is present in the Book of Kells. Man gives to the animals, the birds, the insects, the flowers, the abstract patterns a unity and a cohesion which is overwhelming in its impact. All these varied elements in the illuminator's imagination, drawn from the environment in which he and the other monks of Kells lived and worked, are drawn together by the dominant symbol of Man.

In the Temptation of Christ this sense the artist has of human tension and human destiny provides him with a dramatic picture of the confrontation of Christ and the Devil. In the 'Portrait' of Saint John, on the other hand, the subject is serene and icon-like, the object of veneration and devotion, and any tension there is would be established between this emblem of a Saint and the monks who gazed upon it.

The Books of Kells had a somewhat chequered history. It was stolen in 1007, the gold taken from the shrine in which it was kept, and the book buried 'under a sod'. At the time of the Reformation it was surrendered to the Crown, but before long passed into the hands of Archbishop Ussher, who presented it to Trinity College. It was already defective then, and the book

39

as it stands is in an incomplete state. Yet it is still the richest and most varied of all Irish treasures from the period of Celtic art, and in all its variety and richness of ornament, colour, design, decoration, the very creative imaginations of its scribes and *Ills 21–3* artists, the Book of Kells is itself a concentrated synthesis of those qualities which P. Jacobsthal saw in all the art of the Celtic realms:

> . . . their art also is full of contrasts. It is attractive and repellent; it is far from primitiveness and simplicity; it is refined in thought and technique, elaborate and clever, full of paradoxes, restless, puzzlingly ambiguous; rational and irrational; dark and uncanny – far from the lovable humanity and transparence of Greek art. Yet it is a real style, the first great contribution by the Barbarians to European art, the

21 Book of Kells, Evangelist, early ninth century

22 Book of Kells, Virgin and Child, early ninth century

first great chapter in the everlasting contacts of southern, northern and eastern forces in the life of Europe.

The origins of Celtic art will remain obscure. In its earliest phases it seems to be the abstract expression of man's awareness of himself and his own tangible environment. He is the centre of his own world, and his basic motif is the circle. Then, with the La Tène period, new impulses come in. Perhaps there is Scythian influence on Celtic art. Perhaps there is a very real link between the art which the Scythians brought with them, over a period of generations, from the Khingan Mountains in Mongolia right across Asia to the shores of the Black Sea and the valley of the Danube, there to pass on their rich sense of colour, their obsession with animal symbols in their art, to the easternmost, Hungarian fringes of the Celtic world. Certainly the discoveries at Pazyryk would endorse such a view, even if it must always remain highly conjectural. From then on, even if the influences of Roman, Greek, Byzantine, Scandinavian and North African art can increasingly be detected, the development through the early Christian period continues to be one of puzzle and paradox, right up to the peak of Celtic creativity in the eighth and ninth centuries. With the Viking invasion of the mid-ninth century there comes a kind of watershed. The invasion, which was spread over two distinct periods, has been shown in various lights by different historians. As far as art is concerned it can be fairly clearly stated that the destructive and disruptive nature of the prolonged attacks was in no sense total, and the Viking invasion does not represent an unbridgeable chasm. On the other hand, for close on a century and a half there was pillage and destruction throughout the country, and whatever recovery followed in the eleventh and twelfth centuries, the unique structure which had produced the Book *Ills 21–3* of Kells and the Ardagh Chalice was replaced by a very *Ill. 14* different one in which war and bloodshed, with their attendant anxieties and tensions, were to become an increasingly frequent feature.

43

23 Book of Kells, The Devil tempting Christ to cast himself down from the Temple, illumination to Saint Luke, early ninth century

24 The Cross of Muiredach (Monasterboice, Co. Louth), 923 A D

From the Viking invasion to 1700

The Viking invasion of Ireland did not only disrupt the long period of peaceful development in Irish art. It also ushered in close to eight centuries of invasion, civil war, repression, siege, religious intolerance and tyranny. Art suffered first by being either the object of the pagan greed of the Norse invaders, or the victim of their widespread destruction and desecration. But it continued to suffer far more profoundly after the defeat of the Norsemen at the Battle of Clontarf in 1014, due to the fragmentation of Irish society, and the introduction, with the Norman invasion of 1170, of the fundamental and long-lived division of the country into an Anglo-Irish Pale, centred on Dublin, and a Celtic hinterland, with local rulers, usually in dispute with each other or with their Norman or Plantagenet or Tudor rulers. The art of a nation can survive invasion. It can even survive destruction, so long as the artists themselves survive and re-establish themselves and the stable environment needed for their work. But if that environment itself is destroyed or broken up, then the artist becomes isolated and his sense of social involvement and obligation disappears. Any national tradition will disappear, too. Irish art in this period becomes increasingly meagre and fragmentary. Its only continuity is an historic one, and in its wide range of styles, the diverse influences that become apparent, and in its eventual shift from religious to secular environments it reflects the continuous and turbulent evolution of a new and very different society in the country.

The Viking invasions were not, of themselves, sufficient to destroy Celtic art. They began in the mid-ninth century. For a period of forty years, from 875 to 915, there was relative peace, but then the pillage and destruction became widespread throughout the country for almost a century, finally being

45

ended by Brian Boru at Clontarf in 1014. When the invasions began, Ireland already had one very durable art form which was to survive much of the desolation: its sculpture in stone. Already, during the eighth century, the high crosses had developed very considerably from the early simplicity of the Carndonagh Cross in Donegal. The South Cross, Ahenny, is an elaborate work, deeply carved with spirals and interlacings, its outline a pronounced ridge of gadrooning and the point of intersection of the four arms strongly emphasized by semi-circular indentations. The decoration is for the most part abstract, being in the form of interlacings and spirals, though with some animal representation. Such Biblical scenes as there were on the base of the cross have been considerably weathered, but there is almost certainly the representation of the Lions' Den and possibly of Noah's Ark. In spite of this the cross remains one of the most distinctive of all Irish high crosses, its strong outline emphasized by the wheel-head, and the subtlety of the carving emphasized by the deep, bold outline and the depth of the panels of the cross inside its frame.

Ills 9, 25

It belongs to pre-Viking Ireland. Yet it stands at the beginning of a considerable development of style and technique in sculptured high crosses which can be traced through the ninth and tenth centuries, which survived the Norse incursions, and which probably provided the later period of Celtic art, during the eleventh and twelfth centuries, with much-needed inspiration. One of these, the Cross of Muiredach at Monasterboice, has been dated by its inscription to 923, and others are closely related. Perhaps the finest is the Cross of Moone in County Kildare. Its stately appearance contrasts vigorously with the crude and bold carvings of Biblical scenes and figures. Its height is stressed by the smallness of the wheel-head cross at the top, and by the extended pyramid shape of the base. Yet into this graceful framework a teeming world of activity and vitality has been carved by the unknown sculptor. One magnificent panel at the base of the cross contains the twelve Apostles in rows of four, strictly stylized and uniform, their bodies square,

Ill. 24

Ills 26–8

47

25 The South Cross (Ahenny, Co. Tipperary), eighth century

26 The Cross of Moòne
(Ballitore, Co. Kildare),
ninth century

27 The Cross of Moone,
detail of the base

28 The Cross of Moone, detail, Flight into Egypt

their feet turned out, and their faces, wide-eyed and innocent, strangely comic in their sameness of expression. Many scenes are depicted in the panels on the four sides of the cross, including the Temptation of Saint Anthony, the Flight into Egypt and the Figures in the Fiery Furnace. Some panels contain straightforward representations of animals while others revert to the spirals and patterns of earlier decoration. The style adopted by the sculptor is highly distinctive, and the formalized simplicity, an innocent, almost childlike quality, gives to the complete work great unity and strength.

Ill. 28

There may have been a break, during the second period of Viking raids, in the sequence of development in the sculpture of Irish high crosses. The last group of all, which includes the very fine cross at Drumcliff in County Sligo, overlooking the grave of the Irish poet, W. B. Yeats, and crosses at Roscrea in County Tipperary, Tuam in County Galway and Kilfenora in County Clare, show further stylistic change and development, and belong to the period of resurgent Celtic Christianity in the eleventh and twelfth centuries which preceded the arrival of the Normans.

To this period, too, belong many fine crosiers, shrines, crosses and other religious jewellery, as well as some of the more notable architecture, such as the abbeys at Mellifont, Jerpoint, Cashel and Boyle.

The Shrine of Saint Patrick's Bell was made in about 1100 by order of Donal O'Loughlin, King of Ireland (1088–1121), to enshrine the relic of Saint Patrick known as the Bell of the

Ill. 29

Will. The shrine is made of bronze, with gold and silver interlacings in its panels, many of them incorporating animal designs. Large crystal and coloured glass bosses decorate the sides, and at each end the handles are surrounded by ornate filigree tracery. The style echoes the technique used in the

Ills 13–14 Ardagh Chalice and the Tara Brooch, where panels of silver or bronze were deep enough to contain the richer and far finer gold filigree decoration. The shrine is by no means as intricate as those earlier creations, but it does have a pleasing unity of design, and in places, as in the working of the beady-eyed birds at the top, displays considerable originality.

A number of crosiers from the eleventh and twelfth centuries have survived. Some are only fragments, others are remarkably

Ill. 30 well-preserved. The Lismore Crosier dates from the beginning of the twelfth century and is inscribed with a prayer for Niall, who was Bishop of Lismore, in County Waterford, from 1090 to 1113. The shaft and the crook are of bronze, with decorative panels which at one time probably held filigree designs in gold. There are coloured glass studs on the shaft with cross designs on them, and much of the surface of the crosier was at one time heavily gilded. The curved back of the crook has an openwork crest of animals, intertwined, and with interlacing between them. The crest terminates in the head of an animal at the back, and on the other side of the shaft there is a gilded human head, possibly representing the bishop for whom the crosier was made.

The most glorious creation of this period, however, is the

Ills 31–2 Cross of Cong, which in many of its details recaptures some of the best qualities of eighth-century Celtic art. The cross is a shrine for a fragment of the True Cross, and was made in about 1123 on the orders of the High King of Ireland, Turlough O'Connor. It has various inscriptions, one of the most interesting being a reference to the craftsman who made the cross, Maelisu. It is, in fact, remarkable that the four names related together by the four inscriptions should be those of the king, two bishops and the artist. Yet nothing more is known of Maelisu, and no other work from his inspired hands is recorded.

29 Shrine of Saint Patrick's Bell, *c.* 1100

30 The Lismore Crosier, early twelfth century

Ills 31–2 The cross is of oak cased in copper and silver, and with decorations in gold and gilt bronze. In the centre, and raised from the surface of the cross, is a large quartz crystal behind which the relic was probably encased. But the most striking feature is the point at which the cross is joined to the shaft. The shaft terminates in a large boss decorated with panels of filigree, glass insets and enamel. Out of the top of the boss there emerges a grotesque head which grasps the base of the cross in its teeth. It is a two-sided head, with eyes and prominent ears on both top and bottom, and richly decorated with patterns of scales, spirals and lines. It is the most distinct single feature of the cross, and a remarkable tribute, after a development over many centuries, to the strength of the animal motif in Celtic art in Ireland.

The whole of the front of the Cross of Cong is divided into panels, each filled with gold filigree patterns employing animal designs. These are subtle and delicate, and in some ways quite close to the animal interlacings in the ornamental page of the Ill. 19 Lichfield Gospels. At key points between the panels, and around the outside of the cross, there are small glass and enamel bosses. The sides are covered in silver, and the back of the cross had four long panels of bronze animal interlacings, one of which is now missing. The various inscriptions are engraved in the silver sides of the cross.

In spite of the richness of ornamentation, however, the overall effect of the cross is sombre, even a bit austere. The focus of attention is the single 'eye' of rock crystal, and the balance is such that all other elements are subordinate. This is natural enough. The art reflects a more sophisticated community with a more carefully worked out scale of values. The rich and some-times riotous profusion of an earlier age has been scaled down and disciplined, and if it has lost some originality it has, at the same time, gained in formal consistency and control.

The new sophistication in the structure of Irish communities, with their balanced amalgamation of church and state, the king and bishop whose names are recorded, along with that of the

31 MAELISU The Cross of Cong, *c.* 1123

32 The Cross of Cong, detail of the shaft

artist, on the Cross of Cong, is reflected in the architecture of the period. While the Viking invasions can be regarded as a profound interruption, and the first of many, they were followed, it must be remembered, by a period of relative peace from Brian Boru's victory over the Norsemen in 1014 up to the Norman invasion in 1170, a space of more than 150 years. During that time religious communities of considerable size and influence were established, and the churches which they built are fine and impressive, often surrounded by extensive community buildings, and by the characteristic Round Towers, although these are often of earlier date.

Ill. 32 Mellifont Abbey was the earliest of the Cistercian Houses in Ireland. It was founded by Donagh O'Carroll, King of Oriel, in 1142, and the consecration of the abbey church was attended by Gelasius, the Irish Primate, and by the Papal Legate, Cardinal Paparo, as well as by seventeen bishops and lay leaders from all parts of the country. Four years after the consecration, Boyle

Ill. 34 Abbey, in County Roscommon, was settled from Mellifont. The lofty and impressive church stands on the north side of the town on the banks of the Boyle River. The nave, choir, transepts and massive central tower still stand, as well as some of the domestic buildings. The building is of the Transition Period, and one of the largest built by the Cistercians in Ireland. At Cashel, in County Tipperary, from the fourth to the beginning of the twelfth century the seat of the Kings of Munster, various buildings and ruins bear witness to the chequered fortunes of Irish religious communities during this period. The site contains a tenth-century tower in perfect

Ill. 35 condition, the twelfth-century chapel built by Cormac, King-Bishop of Cashel from 1122 to 1138, the ruins of a cathedral built in 1169, the late eleventh-century Cross of Saint Patrick and various fourteenth- and fifteenth-century additions. Close to the Rock of Cashel, on which these ruins stand, there is a thirteenth-century Dominican friary, and Hore Abbey, a thirteenth-century Cistercian House, again settled from Mellifont in 1266.

54

33 Mellifont Abbey ruin, general view, founded 1142

Mellifont was also the place chosen by King Henry II, on his visit to Ireland in 1172, to receive the homage of the northern chiefs. The occasion underlines the fact that the church now becomes a somewhat neutral onlooker · in the prolonged struggles and disputes between the local chiefs and their English conquerors. Already, in architecture, in sculpture, in manuscript illumination and in the later jewellery and metal-work, foreign influences have become widespread. With the Norman invasion reaching Ireland it is, where art is concerned, a question of more and deeper influences to be added to an already extensive list. The strong Celtic art, which earlier had

34 Boyle Abbey (Co. Ros-common), founded 1146

35 Cashel Cormac's Chapel (Co. Tipperary), consecrated 1134

absorbed with little trace such hints of Mediterranean art as reached the Irish shores, is much weaker in the eleventh and twelfth centuries, and continues to be changed and modified with the spread of Norman and English influences through the country. The continuity is provided by the church. And the Cistercian, Dominican and Franciscan Orders developed their styles of architecture along with all the other aspects of their mission in accordance with the changing society they served. The Cistercians continued to establish Houses up to the fifteenth century, when Holy Cross, in County Tipperary, was built. And the Franciscans followed the same path, building Quin Abbey in County Clare also in the fifteenth century. At that time, too, a cloister was added to the late twelfth-century *Ill. 36* Cistercian abbey of Jerpoint, in County Kilkenny, and decorated with standing figures which show the very considerable change in artistic direction in church sculpture.

The same development can be seen in metalwork. The *Ill. 37* Ballylongford Cross, which was made in 1479 for Cornelius O'Connor of Kerry, belongs to a tradition quite different from *Ills 31–2* that which produced the Cross of Cong. English and Continental influences can be seen in the treatment of the figure of Christ, in the foliate decorations around the edge, and in the replacement of detailed patterns by an extensive inscription on the arms of the cross. The base of the cross is joined to the shaft by means of a swelled, cushion-shaped boss surrounded by diamond-shaped knobs. The device is almost identical to the swelling halfway *Ill. 38* up the stem of the De Burgo-O'Malley Chalice, and this would suggest a connection between the craftsmen responsible for the two works. The Chalice was made some fifteen years after the cross, in 1494, on the orders of Thomas de Burgo and Graunia ni Maile, and is in silver-gilt. In style it follows no native tradition. Similar chalices are to be found in Sweden, and five that are very close in style are at Aston-by-Sutton in Cheshire, Nettlecomb in Somerset, Coombe Keynes in Dorset, Corpus Christi College, Oxford, and the Royal Scottish Museum in Edinburgh.

58

36 Jerpoint Abbey (Co. Killkenny), carved monks in the cloister,
late twelfth century

37 The Ballylongford Cross, 1479

This same alien nature can be detected in the carved figures of the fifteenth century, among the earliest carved wood sculpture known in Ireland. The carved figure of God the *Ill. 38* Father from Fethard is distinctly Spanish in style, although it was probably made in Ireland under foreign influence. The carved wood figure of the Clonfert Madonna, which is some-what earlier, belongs also to a European convention, as does the other Fethard figure of Christ on Calvary and the carving of Saint Molua at Killaloe.

Throughout the fifteenth century, English rule in Ireland continued to fluctuate according to the strength and ability of the King's Deputy. With the accession of Henry VIII new inroads were made which led to the assumption by the king of the title of Supreme Head on Earth of the Church in Ireland following the Reformation, and a death-blow was dealt to the great centres of Irish art, culture and learning with the dissolution of the abbeys and the confiscation of church property.

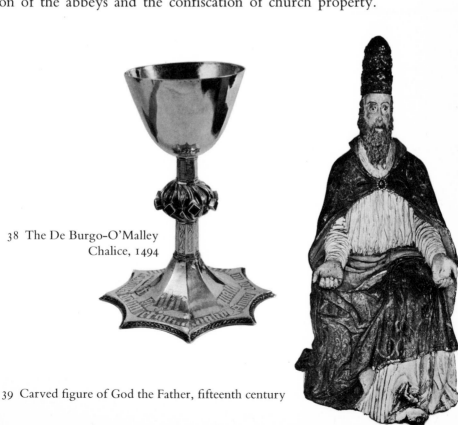

38 The De Burgo-O'Malley Chalice, 1494

39 Carved figure of God the Father, fifteenth century

Almost overnight the art and culture of the country were obliged to find new inspiration, new directions and new practitioners.

They came in two ways: from the urban craftsmen and their guilds, and from the patronage of the ruling classes. Both were directed and influenced from England, and later from the Continent, and both were opposed to what little native art or culture had survived the long periods of civil disturbance. But although alien in inspiration, this new direction in Irish art, the inevitable result of history, was to become as profoundly Irish in its way as any of the earlier influxes of ideas and styles. This was particularly true of the urban groups of craftsmen, the most important and influential of which was the Goldsmiths' Company of Dublin. But the first examples of what is best described as Plantation Art are of a very different sort from the domestic craft of the goldsmith.

Ill. 40   In John Derrick's *Image of Irelande*, published in 1581, are recorded the campaigns of the Lord Deputy, Sir Henry Sidney, and the submission of 'the great O'Neale of Ireland' in 1578. The book contains a remarkable series of woodcuts of which several are signed with initials ID or FD. Possibly the ID refers to John Derrick himself. They are well drawn and vigorous representations of the events of Sir Henry Sidney's rule, the Irish chiefs against whom he was campaigning, his departure from Dublin, his army, drawn up and on the march, a pitched battle, and the capitulation of O'Neale and his followers – with which the book ends. The plates are fine examples of the artist's ability as a draughtsman, and are among the earliest visual records of Irish history and landscape.

The same military situation, though with different protagonists, gave rise to what may be described as the first example of Irish landscape painting, the large *Siege and Battle of Kinsale*, which is in Trinity College, Dublin. It is a military record of the various skirmishes and encounters in and about Kinsale during 1601–2, and in many respects, not least the bird's-eye view of events, it is more a map than a landscape.

40 JOHN DERRICK 'Troops on the March' from *The Image of Irelande*, 1581

Yet it is a picturesque panorama, with a fine sense of perspective, a lively treatment of the encounters between the English on the one hand, and the Irish and the Spanish on the other, with mounted and foot soldiers hurrying about in all directions in the foreground and with the general sense of bustle and activity well conveyed. The artist is unknown, although he is almost certainly the illustrator of Thomas Stafford's *Pacata Hibernia*, published in 1633, and the picture probably dates from that time.

The seventeenth century began with war and rebellion, reached a point of unequalled brutality with the Cromwellian campaign in the early 1650s, and drew to its close amid the Protestant rejoicing which followed the Battle of the Boyne in 1690. During this time the Dublin Goldsmiths' Company was established by Royal Charter from Charles I in 1637, and grew, at first under the influence of Dutch craftsmen working in Dublin, and later with the added impetus of Huguenot craftsmen who settled in Dublin at the end of the century, by which time the standards of craftsmanship were of a very high order.

63

In Cork the goldsmiths formed part of a more general guild, or association of guilds, and the one-time master, Robert Goble, was the goldsmith who made the Mace of the Trade Guilds of the City of Cork, an excellent example of late seventeenth-century provincial Irish work, in which the Dutch immigrant goldsmith, Charles Bekegle, is thought to have had a hand.

A silver tankard made by Edward Swann in Dublin in 1676 is a fine, plain example of the period, bearing the coat of arms of the Fletchers of Chester. Swann was a warden of the Dublin Goldsmiths' Company in 1660, having been made a freeman some six years earlier, and worked on in the city until the 1680s.

Considerable quantities of excellent plate were produced in Dublin during this period. There was an interruption during the Williamite wars, but by 1700, twenty thousand ounces of silver a year were being assayed in Dublin. Some of the best church plate belongs to this second half of the seventeenth century, and towards the end of the century there emerged among Dublin goldsmiths some craftsmen of rare distinction, among them Thomas Bolton, David King and Joseph Walker.

41 JAMES GANDY
Portrait of Frances Molyneux,
Lady O'Neil

In painting this was almost exclusively the age of the portrait. Ireland did not have a rich or sufficiently settled society until well into the eighteenth century for the decorative art which flourished in England, and even the portrait painting of the period is largely the work of anonymous or forgotten artists. Two portrait painters do stand out, however: Thomas Pooley and James Gandy. Gandy (1619–89) came to Ireland under the patronage of the Duke of Ormonde, and was employed doing copies of van Dycks, which in the sale of pictures from Kilkenny Castle as early as 1718 were offered as originals. He was also widely employed as a portrait painter, the majority of his subjects being Jacobites. Three fine examples of his work are at Malahide Castle in north County Dublin, and record the connection between the Irish Jacobite family of Sir Neale O'Neil, a nephew of the Earl of Tyrconnel, and the Molyneux family. There are portraits of Sir Neale, of Caryl, third Viscount Molyneux, and of Frances Molyneux, Lady O'Neil. Gandy is a highly competent and sympathetic portrait painter, whose work has probably been more than decimated by wholesale re-attribution, a hazard found throughout Irish painting of the eighteenth and nineteenth century. Thomas Pooley (1646–1723), whose father was a member of the Irish Bar, lived long enough to be employed on the widely proliferating portraits of William and Mary which followed the Battle of the Boyne. He was also employed by the second Duke of Ormonde to paint portraits of Queen Anne and other members of the royal family which became the property of the Royal Hospital at Kilmainham.

Ill. 41

Ormonde was also responsible, so it is thought, for the visit towards the end of the century of Francis Place (1647–1728), who did a number of important topographical drawings during his stay in Dublin and his travels in different parts of the country. His visit is important for what it tells us, particularly of Dublin, at that time. It is also interesting in being the first of many 'Irish Tours' undertaken by English artists, many of whom were to influence Irish painting and enrich it.

Ill. 42

42 FRANCIS PLACE *View of Dublin from the Liffey Estuary*

The last ten years of the seventeenth century were devoted to the stabilizing of Irish society, and the pattern which emerged by the early 1700s was to remain fairly constant during the next hundred years. Historically the picture, with its exclusively Protestant rule and its Penal Code, is not an attractive one. And it is, perhaps, fortunate that art reflects history only in a very oblique way. The Catholic population of Ireland was deprived, at this time, of the right to participate fully in the social life of the community, and art became a Protestant preserve. Perhaps the greatest irony of all lies in the fact that the Huguenots, themselves Protestant refugees from Catholic oppression, should have established themselves at the heart of many different areas of Irish creative activity at this time.

66

The age of Swift

On the morning of 11 September 1710, Jonathan Swift sat for *Ill. 43*
one of the many portraits painted of him during his lifetime by
the Irish portrait painter, Charles Jervas. At ten o'clock that
evening he wrote to Stella in his *Journal*: 'I sat four hours this
morning to Jervis, who has given my picture quite another
turn, and now approves it entirely: but we must have the
approbation of the town. If I were rich enough, I would get a
copy of it and bring it over.' A month later he was talking of
getting a copy out of Jervas by surreptitious means, through
the agency of a third party. And by 1716, when Jervas was in
Dublin to paint yet another portrait, this time of Swift as Dean
of Saint Patrick's Cathedral, Swift declared himself hard put
to it to avoid the importunate artist. Whatever their relationship developed into, Charles Jervas managed to paint something
in the region of a dozen different versions or copies of Swift's
portrait, probably the best of them being the one in the National
Portrait Gallery in London.

Charles Jervas (1675–1739) was the leading Irish artist of this *Ills 43, 45*
period, and like so many painters who followed him, made his
name as a painter in London. He was a pupil of Godfrey Kneller
for about a year, although not highly regarded by the German
artist who thought little of his ability as a draughtsman. He
then went to Italy, and on his return married a rich widow with
whom he set up house at Hampton. At that time even artists
and writers were split by the political division into Whigs and
Tories, and to some extent Jervas became the artist of the
Tories, while Kneller was busy painting his kit-kat portraits of
the Whigs. Jervas did several portraits of Pope, to whom he
gave lessons in painting, and also portraits of Arbuthnot,
Warburton, Thomas Parnell, Matthew Prior and Joseph

67

Addison, besides a very large number of society portraits. In 1723 Jervas succeeded Kneller as principal painter to George I, and this post was confirmed on the accession of George II. During this period Jervas made at least three fairly extensive trips to Ireland, where he painted a number of portraits, including those of the Archbishop of Dublin, William King, and possibly the portraits of Hester Johnson and Esther Vanhomrigh, Swift's 'Stella' and 'Vanessa', which are in the National Gallery of Ireland.

Jervas was a successful and fashionable painter in his own lifetime, but has since suffered from undeserved neglect. He was a vain man, with immense social aspirations, and his official position obliged him to paint large numbers of portraits of a formal and rather arid kind. Kneller was quite accurate though rather cruel in his condemnation of Jervas's abilities as a draughtsman, as can be seen in the proportions of his otherwise excellent painting of William Augustus, Duke of Cumberland, done in 1727, and now in the National Portrait Gallery. But Jervas painted flesh tones well, and was able to capture a likeness and invest it with life and vigour. A good example of

43 CHARLES JERVAS *Jonathan Swift*

44 HUGH HOWARD *Arcangelo Corelli*

45 CHARLES JERVAS
*Portrait Head of Catherine
Hyde, Duchess of Queensbury*

the artist at his unaffected best may be seen in his *Portrait of a Girl*, with its direct simplicity, its fine flesh tones and straight-forward composition.

Hugh Howard (1675–1737) was born in Dublin in the same year as Charles Jervas and studied painting in Holland and Italy before setting up in Dublin in 1700 as a portrait painter. He worked in the city for fifteen years, and then moved to London, where he married and settled. He was appointed Keeper of the State Papers, and gave up painting. He was a good artist, more flamboyant than Jervas, and a better draughtsman, but with a poor range of colour and a rather gritty texture to his work. His painting of Arcangelo Corelli, with its rococo framework of music and musical instruments, is a rather more entertaining picture than the portraits done of Dublin sitters, many of whom must have been clergymen and Fellows of Dublin University, such as Peter Browne, Provost from 1699 to 1710, whose portrait by Howard is in the Provost's House. Howard is almost certainly responsible for the portrait of his father, Ralph Howard, Regius Professor of Physics (1674–1710), which is also in the college.

Ill. 44

Thomas Carlton (*c.* 1670–1730), James Curry (*fl.* 1730–8), William Payne (*fl.* 1690–1714) and the Stoppelaer family were all working in Dublin at this time as portrait painters. Little is known of Carlton except that he was active in promoting the guild responsible for painters. So also was William Payne. The three Stoppelaers, Charles (*fl.* 1703–45), Herbert (d. 1772) and Michael (*fl.* 1730–75) all painted, Charles probably best of all. A male portrait by him is in the National Gallery of Ireland.

A slightly younger group of portrait painters grew up under the influence of Jervas and Howard. Two of them, Francis *Ill. 49* Bindon and Anthony Lee, were pedestrian painters of no great *Ills 46–8* distinction. The other three, however, Thomas Frye, James *50* Latham and, to a lesser extent, Stephen Slaughter, brought a greater depth and a more flexible style to their portraiture than had been achieved in the earliest years of the century.

James Latham (1696–1747), to judge from his portrait of *Ill. 47* George Berkeley, the philosopher and Bishop of Cloyne, was an artist of very considerable ability. Unfortunately, very few

46 THOMAS FRYE *Portrait of an Artist*

47 JAMES LATHAM *George Berkeley*

of his paintings are known, and much of his work can be judged only from the engravings made from portraits. His Berkeley portrait is a fine work, sympathetic to the character of the man and well painted.

Thomas Frye (1710–62) was an artist of equal distinction, with rare qualities of draughtsmanship and composition in his pictures, although again few of his works are known, partly because his energies were side-tracked into the making of porcelain just at the height of his career and he spent fifteen years running a factory at Bow. Even then he did not return to the painting of portraits, but experimented with mezzotint processes, and published various prints up to his death from consumption in 1762. This was a pity. Frye's abilities as a portrait painter were considerable, as can be seen from his painting of Sir Thomas Wharton, and the fifteen years spent *Ill. 48* making porcelain, which brought him no profit and bad health, interrupted a career of early achievement and great promise. His *Portrait of an Artist* is an intimate and sensitive study in chalk, *Ill. 46*

48 THOMAS FRYE *Sir Thomas Wharton*   49 FRANCIS BINDON *Hugh Boulter*

probably a preliminary sketch for the series of mezzotint heads which he published in 1760. One of these is a self-portrait, and
Ill. 48
is close in style to the oil painting of Wharton.

Ill. 50
Ills 43–5
It is possible that Stephen Slaughter (d. 1765) worked in the studio of Charles Jervas. There are close stylistic similarities, although Slaughter is more wooden in his treatment of figures, concentrating his energies on richly painted draperies and the frequent inclusion of sprays of delicately painted flowers and plants. He worked in both Dublin and London. The identity
Ill. 50
of his *A Lady and Child* is not known.

The only one of these artists to confine his activities almost exclusively to Ireland was Francis Bindon, who died in the same year as Slaughter. He was a portrait painter and an architect, and worked with Richard Castle on Russborough and Belan House. His portraits were many – of Swift alone he did at least eleven – and rather poor, with clumsy technique and muddy colouring. There is a certain rugged honesty in his
Ill. 49
treatment of Hugh Boulter's face, but the rest of this painting of the Archbishop of Armagh, and it is a very extensive work, is undistinguished. The same can be said of his portraits of Swift, which are good, honest likenesses, but which tell us nothing about the man.

Between 1730 and 1750 an important school of engravers was established in Dublin by John Brooks with the assistance of Andrew Miller. Brooks first learnt engraving in Dublin, then went to work for Faber in London. There he met Miller, with whom he returned to his native city to set up a business publishing portraits and views. Brooks and Miller together are important in that they trained in Dublin some of the best eighteenth-century graphic artists in mezzotint, among them James McArdell (1728–65), Charles Spooner (d. 1767), Richard Purcell (d. 1766) and Richard Houston (1721–75), all of them born in Dublin, all pupils to begin with of Brooks, and all destined to achieve considerable reputations working in London in one of the richest but most difficult of graphic media.

The artists who worked in Ireland in the first half of the

eighteenth century were all, to some extent, pioneers. They had the traditions of London to fall back on, or to turn to, and there was quite close liaison between the two capitals. But in Dublin the stability achieved by the victory of William III at the Boyne was a very recent one, and its confirmation by the establishment of Irish *traditions* took time. The most important event in this connection was the foundation of the Dublin Society in 1731 for the purpose of 'improving husbandry, manufacture and the useful arts and sciences'. The Society was modelled on the Royal Society, and did itself become the Royal Dublin Society in 1820. Its first aims were scientific and agricultural, but by 1740 various schemes to aid artists had been started, including a small art school, run by Robert West (d. 1770) and the French artist James Mannin (d. 1779). This, combined with the premiums and awards given for art by the Society, and the purchases made from professional painters and sculptors in order to encourage them, created a vital and significant focus for the arts in Ireland. Most of the important sculptors and painters in Ireland during the eighteenth century were either trained by the Society's schools or benefited from its activities. And all artists could look upon the Society as a

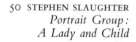

50 STEPHEN SLAUGHTER
Portrait Group:
A Lady and Child

centre at which their work might be exhibited and sold, and from which commissions might be gained.

It is significant that the first awards made by the Dublin Society were for landscape painting, first to Susanna Drury (*fl.* 1733–70) for her watercolours of the Giant's Causeway, which were later engraved, and then, in 1741, to Joseph Tudor (d. 1759). Little is known of Susanna Drury's work except through the engravings, but Joseph Tudor's watercolour drawings of Dublin reveal an artist of considerable ability and output, with a firm line and an excellent sense of perspective. He was probably born in 1695, and his work is the earliest expression of landscape art by an Irish artist working within the rather restricted mode of topographical drawings, many of which were done for engravings, executed by John Brooks and his pupils.

At the same time as Joseph Tudor was working in Dublin, two landscape artists were working in the country, one Italian and one Dutch, both of whom were to have an influence on the art and development of landscape painting. Johann Van der Hagen (*fl.* 1720–45) was an itinerant painter, working much in the south of Ireland, where some of his best paintings, including his *View of the City of Waterford*, were done. He worked for a time in Dublin, and did designs for tapestries for the House of Lords there, as well as working in the theatre at Smock Alley and doing a number of views, one of which, at least, was engraved by John Brooks.

Gabrielle Ricciardelli (*fl.* 1748–77) did not arrive in Ireland until after 1750, but was then a mature artist who immediately made progress, particularly as a painter of topographical views of houses and estates. Few of his works are definitely known, but those that are, and the many almost certain attributions, reveal an able artist, with a distinctive style and composition of his own, a fine understanding of perspective in landscape, a good draughtsman and a painter of very polished technique. A distinctive feature of his work is the generally low position of his horizon and the consequent emphasis he placed on the

74

51 GABRIELLE RICCIARDELLI *Stillorgan Park and Obelisk*

handling of his skies. The painting of Stillorgan Park and
Obelisk, together with at least three other landscapes done
around Dublin, have been for long attributed to Dominic
Serres, although it is now generally agreed that they are all the
work of Ricciardelli. At the end of his life he went to London
and exhibited landscapes there.

Ill. 51

A number of other landscape painters were working in
different parts of the country by the 1740s, many of them
unknown primitives, like the painter of the mural at Mount
Ievers in County Clare or the artist responsible for the view
of Stradbally in County Leix. Both are close in style and

Ill. 52

52 ANONYMOUS *View of Stradbally, County Leix*

53 GEORGE MOORE *View of Westport House*

Ill. 53   composition to the two paintings of Westport House, signed
and dated 'George Moore 1761', but almost nothing is known
of this artist, and the accepted 'portrait map' style of all three
pictures is not sufficient justification for attribution. The
standard of Moore's painting is high, and his colour excellent.

One other important landscape artist of the period is John
Butts (d. 1765), who was born in Cork and taught art by
Ills 54, 56   another landscape painter called Rogers. Both George Barret
Ills 57–8   and James Barry were influenced by Butts, and Barry said of
him, 'His example and works were my first guide and was what
enamoured me with the art itself.' Unfortunately, no certain
landscape by John Butts is now known, in spite of activity in
both Cork and Dublin, and a fair reputation in his lifetime.

Goldsmiths flourished during the first half of the century and
the best Irish silver of all belongs to this period. Men like
Joseph Walker, David King, Anthony Stanley, Thomas Bolton,
Thomas Sutton, Robert Calderwood and Thomas Williamson,
to name only a few out of a host of excellent craftsmen,

produced very fine work. Economic conditions and the time-lag in foreign influence kept much of the work within a simple and sometimes austere stylistic framework, but this tends to enhance the character of the best work, which, like the teapot made by John Clifton in Dublin in 1718, depends on line and shape rather than on decoration. Some excellent work was also produced in Cork, and goldsmiths were establishing themselves in other provincial centres such as Galway and Kinsale. Only after 1730 does Irish silver begin to assume definite and increasing characteristics of its own, with rich if flat-chased rococo decorations, and the full variety and range of this era belong more to the second half of the century.

Many of the styles and decorative techniques which are so well documented in silver appear also in Irish furniture, plasterwork, and the rare examples of Dublin and provincial delftware which have survived. Much of the work reflected the growing prosperity and independence of the country, and it is not surprising that Italian, Dutch and German influence and inspiration should be felt, as well as English stylistic undertones.

54 GEORGE BARRET *On the Dargle*

Ill. 55   The Italian stuccoists, Paul and Philip Francini, were probably responsible, directly or through their pupils and followers, for the greater part of all Irish plasterwork. In furniture the names of few cabinet-makers have survived, although stylistic idiosyncrasies have established a definite and fairly rich tradition, much of it provincial in manifestation. Delftware of a high quality was made in Dublin, Belfast, Limerick and Rostrevor during the middle of the eighteenth century, and in Dublin some really fine ware was produced during the 1750s by Captain Henry Delamain, who was helped by both the Dublin Society and the Irish Parliament. Much of his work is decorated in blue or manganese-purple, and the motifs are often of Chinese origin, although many dishes had landscapes painted on them.

Our information on the art of the first half of the eighteenth century in Ireland is limited, often severely. Many of the most influential artists are known only by a handful of paintings, much of the work is unidentified, there are numerous doubtful and highly speculative attributions, and there are probably many paintings by Irish artists of this period, among them their best works, which are at present masquerading in various collections as the creations of far more illustrious names. Even so, by the 1750s, definite characteristics and trends had become apparent in the arts in Ireland, and there was, through the activities of the Dublin Society, a corporate feeling and a sense of national self-confidence and pride which was to come to an abundant fruition during the second half of the century.

55 FRANCINI BROTHERS
Marcus Curtius

Ireland her own

At a meeting of 'The Club', possibly in Trinity College, in May 1747, Edmund Burke, at that time about nineteen years old, was 'order'd to make a Declamation in praise of painting'. His remarks are summarized in the minute book of 'The Club', which later became the College Historical Society. Burke said:

> That there are three arts, called generally by way of eminence, polite poetry, painting, & musick, that painting is in many things not inferior to poetry, and doubtless superior to Musick, that it gives us all the beauties of nature with the additional pleasure that the mind takes in comparing them & finding their resemblance wth the original, that it greatly tends to the furtherance & improvement of virtue by putting before our eyes the most lively example of the reward of it or the punishment of the contrary. Like St Paul preaching at Athens (a piece of Raphael) it convinces some, astonishes and pleases all. Portraiture particularly useful by showing our Ancestors who have done well, we may be incited to follow their example for wch ends the Romans kept the statues of their ancestors in their houses.

For his remarks Burke 'had the approbation' of the small debating society. Out of those remarks came one of the more influential works on aesthetics of the eighteenth century, *A Philosophical Enquiry into the Origin of our Ideas of the Sublime and Beautiful*. Although the work was not published until 1756, it is generally accepted that it was written a good deal earlier, and in a letter written three nights after the meeting of 'The Club', Burke refers to what could have been the first draft of the work, which he later claimed to have started in his eighteenth year. The essay is unjustly neglected, mainly on account of its basic thesis – a Beethoven–Schubert syndrome for the visual arts – which splits creative works into those which excite ideas of pain or danger, and are therefore sublime, and those which induce love, and are therefore beautiful. But whatever the argument may be about it today, in its own period it was an influential work, admired by Lessing and Kant, and containing within it many of the seeds of Romanticism. It is also of considerable importance in Irish art. Burke was not just a philosopher. He was deeply interested in painting and in painters, and remained so through his life, and he was the patron, friend, and probably the aesthetic guide and teacher of the two most important Irish artists of the second half of the

Ills 54, 56
Ills 57–8
eighteenth century, George Barret (1732–84) and James Barry (1741–1806). Both artists reflect the philosophical ideas contained in *The Sublime and Beautiful* in much if not all of their work, and it could be said of James Barry that a great many of his pictures epitomize Burke's idea of the sublime, particularly
Ill. 58
a painting like *King Lear Weeping over the Dead Body of Cordelia*.

George Barret was the son of a draper, and apprenticed in his youth to a stay-maker. He studied art under Robert West, and won a prize from the Dublin Society at one of the annual exhibitions. For some time he taught drawing, and also coloured prints, and it was probably while Barret was still in his late teens that he met Edmund Burke, four years his senior, who encouraged him to put some of the elder man's philosophical opinions to practical application. Barret did so. For nearly ten years he painted landscapes in the counties of Dublin and Wicklow, and they include some of his best paintings as well as some of his worst exercises in sombre and morbid landscape. In 1762 Barret went to London. He exhibited there a number of his Irish landscapes, and their originality, which derived from first-hand experimentation based on a theory of painting rather than on example, won him a reputation in a fairly short space of time. There are a number of somewhat apocryphal stories about the large sums of money Barret earned from his painting, but it is certain that he was enormously

56 GEORGE BARRET *Powerscourt Waterfall*

popular. He became bankrupt, however, and was rescued towards the end of his life by Edmund Burke, who secured for him the lucrative sinecure of Master Painter to the Chelsea Hospital. Barret was a founder-member of the Royal Academy.

His painting has been unduly neglected, as it was unduly praised in his lifetime, and he is generally dismissed as a rather poor follower of Richard Wilson. Wilson certainly influenced Barret, but not really to Barret's advantage as a painter. Indeed the Irishman's art divides quite clearly into two periods – before and after the encounter with the English painter of classical training and ideals. When Barret arrived in London he was an artist of considerable originality. The only landscape he had experienced was the richly picturesque and varied one of the countryside south of Dublin, and possibly Killarney. This included such venerated tourist spots of the eighteenth century as the Dargle, Powerscourt Waterfall and the mountains and valleys of Wicklow and Dublin. He painted them as he found them, with rich masses of trees and wild waterfalls, little attempt to conventionalize the composition by the introduction of foreground 'framework', and a rapid style and thick impasto which sometimes produced a certain crudity while at the same time giving to his work great vigour and strength. Even in his earliest pictures his treatment of trees was very accomplished, and his sense of light highly effective and unusual. He often painted *into* the light, with dramatic, silhouette effect, and time and again with these early works one is aware of a strikingly original hand and eye, with little more than rudimentary training, being applied to landscape, and achieving a distinctive and powerful interpretation which at different times must have satisfied both of Burke's theoretical requirements.

Ills 54, 56

After London and Wilson, Barret becomes a dull and rather conventional painter. Technically he improved. His later canvases are smooth and harmonious in colour, texture and composition. But they betray most of the signs of a superficially felt conviction, with their careful framing of the middle ground and distance by foreground foliage, trees to left and right, and the traditional figure of shepherd or cowherd in the corner, with his dog and his beasts. And the light itself in these works, a golden, classical suffusion over everything, while technically law-abiding, lacks the fine sharpness and character to be found in his early works.

Barret probably lacked the sort of self-confidence needed to preserve his artistic character and independence in the highly competitive environment of London in the 1760s. His early success and the frequent commissions which followed it demanded a fluent and fairly rapid style which could be easily varied and repeated, and adapted where necessary to the kind of views which his clients asked for. From Wilson's carefully developed classicism Barret appears to have taken the rudiments and developed them into a sound but fundamentally arid and superficial art with which he then replaced the far richer and more extensive style of his youth. The fault is one to which many Irish artists have succumbed in their graduation from Ireland to London, if indeed it can always be called a fault. The irony is that Barret is almost always judged on his late, mature work, and not unnaturally found wanting, while his early paintings, with their originality of style, composition and light are generally ignored. And this basic dichotomy is further complicated by the fact that Barret was too good an artist not to be continually improving and refining his technical ability; where he found in himself a lack, as with figures and animals, he was not above calling in the help of various other artists, including Sawrey Gilpin, George Stubbs and Philip Reinagle, the latter two of whom were responsible for the figures and animals in *A View Looking East towards Knipe Scar from Lowther Park*.

James Barry was a very different kind of artist. He was a *Ills 57–8* Catholic, the son of a bricklayer, and was born in a small cottage in Cork. He went to sea at an early age, but soon gave it up and devoted his time to art. He was influenced by the Cork landscape artist, John Butts, and at the age of twenty-two, in 1763, he went to Dublin, where he was awarded a prize by the Dublin Society for his *Saint Patrick Baptising the King of Cashel*. He came to the attention of Edmund Burke, and in the following year went to London with him and was introduced to Reynolds and other leading English artists of the time. At this stage Burke was a good deal more influential than when he had met Barret in the early 1750s, and it is not unreasonable to imagine that his effect on Barry was a good deal more profound and long-lasting. At the same time it was probably as bad for Barry as it was good for Barret. Burke was a man who believed in the superiority of the emotions over the intellect, and this belief is at the root of his aesthetics. In leading Barry towards an

57 JAMES BARRY *Adam and Eve*

attempt on the sublime in art – and Burke is at least partially
responsible for this – he was placing the Cork artist on a line of
development for which he was technically ill-equipped; and
from his arrival back in England in 1771, after working and
studying art in Rome for five years, until his death in 1806,
Barry's powers of visual composition, his draughtsmanship, his
handling of paint, even so elementary a thing as his understanding of human anatomy, could not match the range of his
imagination and vision. There is a touch of absurdity in many of
his paintings which results directly from this, and which
reaches an almost ridiculous level in some of the large wall
paintings done for the Royal Society of Arts from 1777 to 1783.
Ill. 57   Barry's *Adam and Eve* avoids the more obvious pitfalls, but even
so is limited by more mundane considerations. Redgrave says

84

58 JAMES BARRY *King Lear Weeping over the Dead Body of Cordelia*

that it 'evinces no feeling for colour, and even the forms are inelegant, unduly round, and without interior markings, their pose somewhat stiff, and the action not easy'. It was exhibited in London in 1771, and the following year Barry became an Associate of the Royal Academy, gaining full membership in 1773.

As well as working on the wall paintings for the Royal Society of Arts, Barry painted several portraits, including at least one of Edmund Burke, and a number of self-portraits which reveal much about his character. His tongue and his temper made him many enemies, lost him the RA Professorship of Painting and eventually brought about his expulsion. Perhaps the extent of the gap between his ambition and his achievement can be best seen in *King Lear Weeping over the*   *Ill. 58*

85

Dead Body of Cordelia. It is difficult but not impossible to understand the sort of mind that could attempt such a work. William Blake was one such, but with a far finer range of colour and ability of draughtsmanship. The Lear picture is inevitably a failure, but perhaps it is a noble one.

Barry was an historical painter before his time, and one who attempted to infuse his work with elements of the sublime to an excessive degree. Effective historical painting was to wait, at least as far as Irish art was concerned, for the balanced and technically brilliant work of Daniel Maclise during the 1830s and 1840s. Landscape, on the other hand, developed rapidly with the work of a considerable group of artists including Jonathan Fisher, John James Barralet, Thomas Sautelle Roberts, James Malton, Nathanial Grogan, a group of lesser topographical artists, and an important and influential visitor from England, Francis Wheatley.

Francis Wheatley (1747–1801) was a London artist and a pupil of Richard Wilson's. He was already a Society of Arts prize-winner at the age of fifteen, and established a practice as a painter quite early, concentrating on small full-length portraits and conversation pieces, as well as landscapes in watercolour. He made his first visit to Ireland before he was twenty, and did some landscapes which were then shown in London. In 1779 Wheatley returned to Dublin, this time to avoid his London creditors, and stayed in Ireland until 1784, a period marked by some of his most important paintings, and a period during which his probable influence on Irish topographical artists like Malton and Fisher was considerable. Wheatley is at his most delightful in rustic or arcadian landscapes, whether in watercolour or oil. His *Nymphs Bathing, a View of the Salmon Leap at Leixlip* is a perfect example of his smooth and relaxed technique, his excellent colours and clever composition. He painted water, foliage and human figures with great proficiency, and numerous watercolours of great beauty indicate the range of his ability in this medium. He was also a portrait painter of distinction. Some of his portraits seem rather

59 FRANCIS WHEATLEY *Nymphs Bathing, a View of the Salmon Leap at Leixlip*

stilted because of the attempt to combine them with landscapes,
as in the *Review of Troops in Phoenix Park, 1781* and the portrait
of Admiral Arthur Phillip, both in the National Portrait
Gallery. In the same Gallery are a spirited self-portrait, and a
painting of the elderly Henry Grattan.

But Wheatley's most significant work was the historical
painting done in Ireland, including his *View of College Green,*
with a Meeting of the Volunteers, on 4th November, 1799 and his
painting of *The Irish House of Commons, 1780.* Wheatley
handles these large subjects with the same ease and balance that

Ill. 60

60 FRANCIS WHEATLEY *View of College Green, with a Meeting of the Volunteers, on 4th November, 1779*

he applied to much smaller works. He gives as much vigour and reality as possible to what is basically a collection of cameo portraits and a journalistic record of an 'event', and he paints it with his usual skill and harmony. He left debts behind him in Ireland in 1784, just as he had left them in England five years earlier, and the remaining seven years of his life were spent in London.

Ill. 61   It is likely that Wheatley not only influenced James Malton (d. 1803) but also gave him practical help with the drawing of some of the figures in his Views of Dublin, although Malton was also helped in this respect by Robert Smirke and by Barralet. Malton started out as a draughtsman in the offices of *Ills 77–8* the architect, James Gandon, during the building of the Custom House in Dublin. He did a number of early watercolours, many of them copies of Paul Sandby, and he seems to have painted quite widely in England before coming to Dublin. Most of his drawings in the British Museum date from the 1780s. But Malton's greatest work, on which he spent ten years of his life,

61 JAMES MALTON *Front View of Trinity College, Dublin*

was his collection of Views of Dublin which were drawn in *Ill. 61*
1790–1, and published in parts during the following eight
years. They are the finest views of Dublin ever done, and they
rank with the best topographical views in Ireland or England
at that period. The twenty-five views were engraved in
etching and aquatint. Malton issued two trial views in 1790,
one of the Custom House and one of the Parliament House, in
the latter of which two pigs were drawn, but later removed in
the published plate of 1793. It is generally believed that objec-
tions were raised to the pigs by members of the Irish Parliament.
Regular publication began in Dublin and London in 1792. The
plates were worked from watercolour drawings by Malton
himself, and were printed in sepia and in black. Coloured sets
were issued, the hand-colouring generally done on sepia plates,
and they were so popular that printings of the views continued
up to the 1820s, by which time the plates had become extremely
worn. As well as the original watercolours Malton did watercolour copies, and he also coloured in outline etchings, probably

89

as guides to the colourists he employed. The views are principally architectural in style, although he did capture much of the atmosphere of the city at that time. In the early 1790s, after taking the views but before publishing any of them, Malton left Dublin for London where he spent the rest of his life. He committed suicide in 1803.

Jonathan Fisher (d. 1809) was, like Barret, the son of a draper, and a self-taught artist. He was a painter of topographical landscapes, and spent most of his life painting views in Ireland which were then engraved, the early ones by engravers employed by Fisher working in line, the later series of sixty *Ill. 62* plates in his *Scenery of Ireland* aquatinted by the artist himself, and published in 1796. Fisher's painting of the Lower Lake, Killarney, was later engraved, as were almost all his works in oil.

Fisher was a competent but rather dull artist. His landscapes are accurate, with good perspective and well-painted skies, but the monotony of mountains and water is rarely relieved by good foregrounds or the interest of figures.

62 JONATHAN FISHER *View of the Lower Lake, Killarney*

63 WILLIAM ASHFORD *The Casino at Marino, near Dublin*

While Malton and Fisher worked largely on their own, there were several collections of views in Ireland which brought together many of the landscape artists. Thomas Milton (1743–1827) engaged a number of them to do watercolour drawings for his *Views of Seats in Ireland* and Francis Grose (1731–91) employed several Irish artists to work on his *Antiquities of Ireland* in the 1790s. The artists included William Ashford (1746–1824), William Purs (1742–82), John James Barralet (1747–1815), Thomas Sautelle Roberts (1760–1826), Francis Wheatley, Jonathan Fisher and Angelo Maria Bigari (*fl.* 1772–9), as well as others.

Ill. 63
Ill. 64
Ills 59–60
Ill. 62

William Ashford is the most important of these artists. He was born in Birmingham and settled in Dublin at the age of eighteen. From the 1760s until 1821 he exhibited regularly, and lived on to see the Royal Hibernian Academy established with himself elected as its first President in 1823. He did a number of

Ill. 63

large landscapes in and around Mount Merrion for Lord Fitzwilliam in the early 1800s, and these, together with some of his drawings, are in the Fitzwilliam Museum in Cambridge. At about the same time he probably completed his painting of

Ill. 63 the Marino Casino, one of his finest works. Large canvases suited his style, which was open and expansive, and which combined good light and skies with well composed foregrounds. Sometimes his figures are weak, but they are rarely a dominant feature.

John James Barralet learnt his art in the Dublin Society schools, set up in London for a while and exhibited there, and then returned to Dublin where he painted, mostly in sepia and watercolour. He eventually left Dublin, and spent the last part of his life in Philadelphia. He was a fine and sensitive artist, and

Ill. 64 his sepia drawing, *Ruins of Ringsend Bridge, Dublin*, shows his excellent handling of figures, rock and water. Barralet worked with Bigari and Gabriel Beranger (1729–1817), but was considerably better than either of them as a draughtsman. Also working at the same time were Thomas Walmsley (1763–1806), who published several views of Irish landscape in coloured aquatint; James George Oben (or O'Brien, *fl.* 1779–1819), an obscure but highly competent watercolourist; Robert Crone (d. 1779), another obscure landscape painter of a slightly earlier period; and Nathaniel Grogan (*c.* 1740–1807), a Cork artist who travelled widely but did most of his best work in County Cork. Finally among landscape artists of the period there are the two Roberts brothers, Thomas (*c.* 1749–78) and Thomas Sautelle. Four fine landscapes of parklands by the elder Roberts are at Leixlip Castle; they are smooth and open in style, broad in composition and with good if subdued colouring. His younger brother worked in a much more fulsome style, painting animals with greater freedom and vigour, using colour more freely, and composing his landscapes with more variety and sense of contrast. In this he represents to some degree the changeover from the eighteenth to the nineteenth century, the movement from accurate topographical landscape to the art

92

64 JOHN JAMES BARRALET *Ruins of Ringsend Bridge, Dublin*

of the picturesque, and is as easy to place in the nineteenth century, with his friends Comerford and Cuming, as in the closing years of the eighteenth.

Many portrait painters were working in Ireland during the second half of the eighteenth century, but perhaps three names stand out above the rest: Nathaniel Hone (1718–84), Horace *Ills 65–6, 67* Hone (1756–1825) and Hugh Douglas Hamilton (1739–1808). *Ills 68–9*

93

Each worked in a different medium. Nathaniel Hone was an enamelist and portrait painter in oils. At his straightforward best he was an excellent artist. His portrait of John Camillus, his youngest surviving son, is a delightful piece of work.

Ill. 66 Called *The Piping Boy*, it is inspired by affection and sympathy, and is painted with simplicity and directness. The portrait of John Wesley in the National Portrait Gallery is another fine painting, and so is the portrait there of 'Kitty' Fisher, the unfinished half-length of Horace Walpole and the self-portrait. He painted a number of these, perhaps the best of which is the one in London, although there is a good self-portrait in the

Ill. 65 Manchester City Art Gallery. They all reveal a rather proud and aggressive man, and not without justification. Hone engaged in a number of rows, one of which resulted in his painting the ill-conceived and badly executed picture, *The Conjuror*, in which he ridiculed Angelica Kauffmann, and which was thrown out of the Royal Academy exhibition. It is now in the

65 NATHANIEL HONE *Self-portrait*

66 NATHANIEL HONE *The Piping Boy*   67 HORACE HONE *Mrs Siddons*

National Gallery of Ireland. Hone also painted a number of miniatures. Both of his sons, Horace and John Camillus, were artists, as well as his brother, Samuel, with whom he had a close physical resemblance.

Horace Hone was unquestionably the finest Irish miniature painter, and by any standards a miniaturist of great talent. He learnt from his father, and exhibited his work in London before setting up in Dublin in 1782. In the following year Mrs Siddons made her first appearance at the Smock Alley Theatre, and in 1784 Hone did his fine portrait of her, with its poignant expression and softness in the features, conveyed with an extreme delicacy of touch. His self-portrait, in the National Gallery of Ireland, is an accomplished miniature, and so is his portrait of Charles, Duke of Rutland, Lord Lieutenant of Ireland. Hone was a prolific artist, both during the period in Dublin, and later, after his return to London where he continued working for a further twenty years.

Ill. 67

Hugh Douglas Hamilton devised his own style of portraiture in pastel, became very skilful at it, and enjoyed a long and successful career doing portraits which are halfway between miniatures and full canvas paintings. They are finely drawn in black, white and coloured chalks, usually about ten by eight inches, good likenesses, with expressive and lively appearances, good handling of eyes, hair and flesh, and a kind of restrained freshness in them which is most attractive. He worked for six years in Dublin, and then went to London, where he was equally successful. His portrait drawings vary little, yet they never seem to lose the charm and spontaneity of a good likeness

Ill. 68 taken at one sitting. His portrait of Walter Hussey Burgh is a good example of his work. In 1778 he went to Italy and settled in Rome where he stayed for twelve years. He came under the not too happy influence of Flaxman, who persuaded him to attempt more ambitious subjects. This resulted in work like his

Ill. 69 *Cupid and Psyche in the Nuptial Bower*, although this was probably completed after his return to Dublin in 1791, where he continued his practice, doing many more portraits in oils,

96

until his death in 1808. These last works are very fine and include leading Irishmen of the period, John Philpot Curran, Lord Edward FitzGerald, Viscount Kilwarden and a fine head of the Irish banker, David La Touche, a man he had drawn in chalk twenty or so years earlier. All these works are in the National Gallery of Ireland which has the best collection of Hamiltons in existence.

69 HUGH DOUGLAS HAMILTON *Cupid and Psyche in the Nuptial Bower*

70 THOMAS HICKEY *An Actor between the Muses of Comedy and Tragedy*

A number of other portrait painters and miniaturists worked during this period. Thomas Hickey (1741–1824) began like Hamilton working in chalk, and produced a very early and competent portrait of Charles Lucas, in black and white crayon on grey paper, which is in the National Gallery of Ireland. He then progressed to portraits in oils, often of groups, and to theatrical paintings, including his *An Actor between the Muses* *Ill. 70* *of Comedy and Tragedy*. It is a rather stilted picture and over-dramatized, a fault which his portraits also suffer from. He later visited India and China, and the pictures he did there have a certain distinction and charm, although they remain a bit lifeless.

Francis Robert West (1749–1809) was the son of the first master of the Dublin Society's school, and was taught by his father. He also worked in pastel, and there are some pleasing portrait drawings in the National Gallery of Ireland, but not of any great distinction. Jeremiah Barrett (d. 1770) seems to have *Ill. 71* been an itinerant portrait painter of the middle years of the eighteenth century, working in the west of Ireland as well as Dublin. His portraits were said to be good likenesses, and he had a firm and unpretentious style. Robert Fagan (1745–1816) was a Cork artist who lived in Rome and Naples, and painted a number of portraits there. His figures are strongly drawn, but a bit wooden. In 1780 Robert Home (1752–1834) arrived in Dublin, and for ten years flourished in the city as a portrait painter. He was commissioned by Trinity College to paint a series of full-length portraits, including Burke, Swift, Berkeley, King and Ussher. The only one done from life was the portrait of Henry Grattan, and this seems to have disappeared. Home's arrival in the city deprived Robert Hunter (*fl.* 1752–1803) of *Ill. 72* work. Hunter, who came from the north of Ireland, was in many ways a more honest and sympathetic painter. His large, full-length portrait of Nicholas, Lord Taaffe, is an excellent piece of work, and his portrait of the Irish composer, Francis

71 JEREMIAH BARRETT
Anne Gore, Countess of Altamont

72 ROBERT HUNTER
Francis Hutcheson

73 THOMAS ROBINSON *The Entry of Lord Hardwick into Belfast as Lord Lieutenant, 27th August 1804*

Ill. 72   Hutcheson, is well painted. It was at first thought to be a portrait of the composer's father, the philosopher of the same name. In his turn Robert Home's position as the leading portrait painter in Dublin was usurped by the arrival in 1789 of the American portrait painter, Gilbert Charles Stuart (1755–1828), who practised in the city with great success for four years. A number of his portraits are in the National Gallery of Ireland, but his influence was probably marginal. There were two other painters in the north of the country at this time, Joseph Wilson (*fl.* 1770–1800) and Thomas Robinson (d. 1810). Robinson actively associated himself and his art with the early development of Belfast, and his most important painting, *The Entry of*

Ill. 73   *Lord Hardwick into Belfast as Lord Lieutenant, 27th August 1804* was done there the year before Trafalgar. Wilson worked in Belfast and in Dublin, and a number of his portraits are in the Ulster Museum.

100

The development of sculpture in Ireland during the second half of the eighteenth century was primarily a result of the work of John Van Nost and Simon Vierpyl, and the financial encouragement of the Dublin Society. John Van Nost (d. 1787) came to Dublin in about 1750 from London where his father was a sculptor of some note. He had a virtual monopoly in the city, and completed several important works, including the equestrian statue of King George II shown in Malton's view of St Stephen's Green, as well as numerous portrait busts. Simon Vierpyl (1725–1810) came under the patronage of Lord Charlemont but confined his work mostly to stone carving and did little statuary. He was employed on the decoration of the Marino Casino shown in William Ashford's landscape, and did a few portrait busts which are in Trinity College. Patrick Cunningham (d. 1774) was the first Irish sculptor of note. He was apprenticed to Van Nost by the Dublin Society and did some portrait work, including a bust of William Maple, but he

Ill. 74

Ill. 75

74 JOHN VAN NOST *Thomas Prior*   75 PATRICK CUNNINGHAM *William Maple*

76 EDWARD SMYTH Carved head
representing the River Bann

spent much of his time doing wax modelling, which sold better,
and the greater part of his output is now lost. But Simon
Vierpyl had in his apprentice, Edward Smyth (1749–1812), a
far more versatile and significant artist. Smyth, son of a stone-
cutter, was employed in the same capacity by Darley, an
Ills 77–8 employee in turn of Gandon's, the architect of the Custom
House. Gandon was greatly impressed by Smyth's work, and
Ill. 76 employed him, not only for the sculptures on the Custom
House, but on all his Dublin building. Much of his work has
weathered, but the fine set of heads representing the rivers of
Ireland which decorate the Custom House indicate an artist of
considerable vigour and originality. Two other sculptors of
note belong to this period, John Hickey (1751–95) and
Christopher Hewetson (1739–99). Much of Hickey's work was
in the form of monuments in churches, the finest of which are
in St Peter's Church, Drogheda, to Henry Singleton; in
Delgany Church, to David La Touche; and in St Helen's

77 JAMES GANDON The Custom House, Dublin

Church, Abingdon, to Mrs Hawkins. Hewetson's best work is the Baldwin Monument in the Theatre at Trinity College. He did some portrait busts, including one of the Duke of Gloucester in 1772, at Windsor.

The second half of the eighteenth century was one of the most prosperous and exciting periods in Ireland, and it was fortunate that the prosperity, together with the growth and expansion of Dublin which resulted from it, should have come at a time when taste and style in all things, but particularly in architecture, were capable of producing a whole range of buildings, both public and private, which were not only fine and impressive, but memorable, and on occasion inspired.

78 JAMES GANDON The Four Courts, from the Merchant's Quay, Dublin

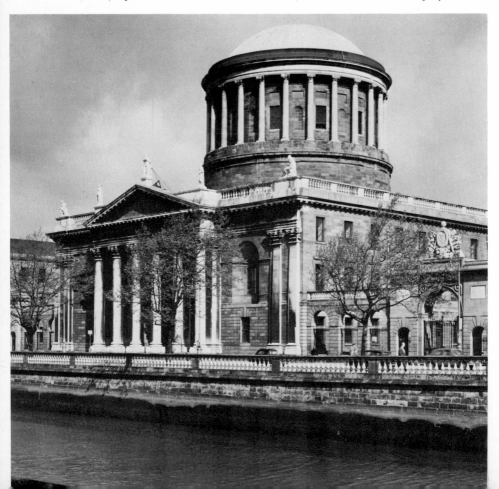

The chief architect of the period was James Gandon (1743–1824), responsible for two great Dublin buildings, the Custom *Ills 77–8* House and the Four Courts, as well as other work. Gandon was born in London, and studied under Sir William Chambers – himself the architect of important buildings in Ireland. He did a number of quite important works in London before being invited to Ireland to build a new Custom House in 1781. The work took him ten years, cost £300,000 and was attended by various difficulties over labour, material and vested opposition to moving the main centre of commerce down river by half a mile from the site of the previous custom house. But the building, when finished, became one of the chief glories of the city, and is still among the finest examples of eighteenth-century architecture in the British Isles.

Gandon went on to design the Four Courts, another splendid example of Irish architecture during this period, the King's Inns in Henrietta Street, Carlisle (now O'Connell) Bridge and the alterations to the Parliament House carried out in 1785.

Richard Cassels (d. 1751) belongs to an earlier period than Gandon. He was a German architect who was brought to Ireland by Sir Gustavus Hume to rebuild a house in Fermanagh. He settled in Dublin and was successfully employed on various buildings in the city, including the dining hall and the very attractive printing house in Trinity College. But his chief work was Leinster House, now the seat of Government, but originally the town house for the Earl of Kildare. It is a fine, stately house, somewhat hemmed in now by subsequent additions to the building complex in the area and much altered inside, but externally a superb example of the architect's style. Cassels did a large number of private houses in Ireland, on one of which, Russborough, he collaborated with the portrait painter, Francis Bindon.

Sir William Chambers (1726–96) was brought to Ireland by Lord Charlemont and designed a number of important buildings in Dublin, including the Theatre and the Chapel in Trinity College, as well as Charlemont House (now the Municipal

Gallery of Modern Art) and the Casino at Marino, both for his patron. The Casino is a perfect piece of work. It was originally designed as a dwelling on a fairly small scale, but its functional value cannot have been more than a vague consideration with the architect or his patron, who worked closely together on questions of this sort, and both of whom must have regarded this particular building as an example of architecture entirely for its own sake.

But these three architects – Chambers, Cassels and Gandon – for all their involvement in the architectural growth of Dublin, were not Irish, and the style and training which they imposed on their work derived from England and the Continent. There was no strong native tradition, in spite of the attention paid to architecture by the Dublin Society. Even so, a few Irish architects emerged whose work stands up well in comparison with the major buildings for which the country turned – almost inevitably – to London, or even further. Of these Thomas Ivory and Francis Johnston should be mentioned.

Thomas Ivory (d. 1786) was the master of architectural drawing in the Dublin Society schools between 1759 and 1786. He came from Cork, but little is known of his life, and few of his buildings are recorded. His finest work is the Blue Coat School on the north side of the River Liffey. Francis Johnston (1761–1829) belongs to a slightly later period. He had a distinctive style, and among other things was responsible for a series of Irish Georgian castles, some of them original, others additions to existing buildings. Johnston was a busy and successful architect, and much of his work belongs to the nineteenth century, not only in date but to a great extent in style as well, for he was an innovator of considerable originality. He designed the General Post Office in Dublin, burnt but not demolished in 1916, and also the Nelson monument which was blown up in 1966. One of his finest and most distinctive achievements is St George's Church.

Not unnaturally the social and economic situation in Ireland which gave rise to the considerable expenditure on public buildings, and the aesthetic awareness which produced so much interest in the architects chosen for such work, affected buildings from such important structures as the Custom House and the Four Courts right down to those of a more humble domestic nature. There is a balanced character and homogeneity about the residential houses and terraces in Dublin. There is also evidence of the competitive attitude felt by estate owners in the building or rebuilding of their houses during the second half of the eighteenth century and on into the nineteenth. Lord Charlemont, with his close interest in the work of his own architect, Sir William Chambers, is typical of a great number of the nobility and landed gentry, many of whom chose to design for themselves rather than to employ an architect.

Ills 77–8

In Dublin this awareness led to the laying out of the many fine squares and wide streets, and the same thing is reflected to a lesser degree in towns and cities throughout the country. And with the concern for style in the buildings themselves there

Ill. 79

79 JOHN ENSOR Merion Square, Dublin

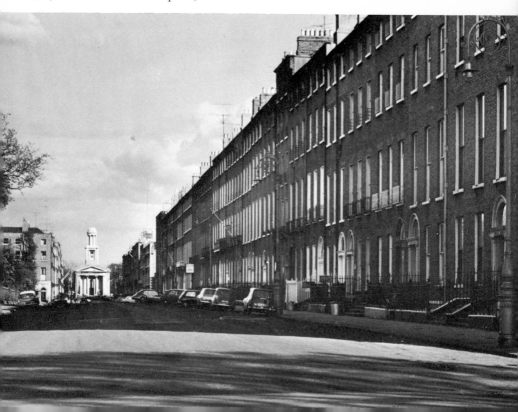

came also a flourishing of interior decoration and adornment. The plasterwork introduced early in the century by Italian craftsmen – notably the Francini Brothers – became a widespread craft in the country, practised by many highly accomplished Irish workers. The same effect was achieved by men like Bossi, who established a tradition in marble-work for fireplaces which was quickly imitated with remarkably good results.

Ill. 55

And in sympathy with this, furniture, glass and silver all reached points of very considerable achievement. Glass factories flourished in Dublin, Belfast, Cork and Waterford, and the output, particularly from Cork and Waterford, was of a very high standard, with individuality of design and technique and with a remarkably successful period of operation, both before and after the Act of Union. And the last part of the eighteenth century saw the richest and most varied styles and designs in Irish silver, with the simple austerity of an earlier age being replaced by arcadian, rococo and bucolic attitudes which reflected not only the influences of Europe and England but also the growing prosperity of Ireland.

Ill. 80

Ill. 81

80 ANONYMOUS
Waterford glass honey jar

81 ANONYMOUS
Pierced dish-cover,
Dublin 1773, silver

Unfortunately, it was short-lived. The historic occasions recorded by Francis Wheatley during his time in Ireland are evidence of the independence of spirit in the country at that time, but they do not reflect the growing discontent of the Catholics, the increasing tension which led to the formation of the United Irishmen and the Orange Order in the 1790s, and the bitter sense of frustration which brought about the Rebellion of 1798, with its bitter reprisals, and its worst result, the Act of Union of 1800. It was a failure made tragic by the fact that the enlightened moderation of Grattan's Parliament and its efforts to broaden the Protestant establishment were betrayed by frustrated idealism on the one hand and stubborn prejudice, political weakness and fear on the other. The results were to affect art no less than they affected the prosperity of Ireland. Yet, as in politics, it is possible to see in the development of art during the nineteenth century a more natural and a more native phenomenon than any that had evolved during the previous hundred years, and while the evolution was difficult and painful, it led finally to some of the best and most Irish artists of all.

Ills 59–60

Landscape into art

In the summer of 1813 three rather bewildered Irish artists arrived in London. The eldest, George Petrie, inspected some of the city's exhibitions and public collections and then returned to Dublin. The other two, Francis Danby and James Arthur O'Connor, set out for Bristol. They arrived there with very little money, and it seems that Danby had to sell two of his watercolours of County Wicklow to pay for their lodging. Danby settled in Bristol, and from there went to London about ten years later. O'Connor returned to Dublin, but only for a few years. He was working in the west of Ireland five years after the visit to London, and thereafter he seems to have spent a great deal of his life travelling about, both in England and on the Continent. He was the least successful of the three artists, dying in near poverty, and he was undoubtedly the best.

Ills 95–6
Ills 82–3

In their destinies these three painters offer a miniature version of the fates of Irish artists throughout the nineteenth century. A number of them went to London. There were various reasons. Since the Act of Union, Dublin had lost much of its social lustre, and London was continually increasing its metropolitan magnetism. Painters like Sir Martin Archer Shee, Daniel Maclise, William Mulready, Samuel Lover, Richard Doyle and Adam Buck all gravitated to the capital, and all made considerable contributions to the areas of art in which they worked. At the same time a rather different group of artists determined to establish and improve their position in Dublin and in the country generally by setting up an Irish academy of painters on the lines of the Royal Academy in London. Artists during the eighteenth century had been well served by the Dublin Society, with its purchases and grants, and its schools in drawing and sculpture and architecture. But it was, in the main,

Ill. 97
Ills 101–6

benevolent patronage from outside, not the corporate work of the artists themselves, and by the time the Dublin Society got round to the idea of holding exhibitions for artists generally, the artists had decided to do it for themselves. They tried various group endeavours during the second half of the eighteenth century and the early years of the nineteenth. The Society of Artists in Ireland was formed in 1765. In 1773 a splinter group set up, calling itself the Academy of Artists. Between 1780 and 1800 there seem to have been no public exhibitions in Dublin, and then in the latter year The Society of the Artists of Ireland was formed only to split in 1812 into The Irish Society of Artists and The Society of Artists of the City of Dublin. These two amalgamated again in 1814 into The Hibernian Society of Artists, which a year later divided once more into The Artists of Ireland and The Hibernian Society, only to come together yet again in 1816, and to hold joint exhibitions under the auspices of the Dublin Society until that society closed down its exhibition premises when it purchased Leinster House. This rather Irish state of affairs was ended in 1823 by the formation of the Royal Hibernian Academy. William Ashford was its president, and among its *Ill. 63* founder members were Martin Cregan, William Cuming, J.G. and T.J. Mulvaney, Joseph Peacock, Thomas Sautelle Roberts and William Mossop, the medallist. Three years later Petrie was made an associate member, and in 1828 a full member. The RHA will be mentioned again, but it is worth pointing out at this stage that throughout the nineteenth century, and for the greater part of the twentieth, the Academy, in spite of neglect, disagreement and a schism in the 1850s not unlike the many group rivalries of the period 1800–20, has been at the centre of artistic activity in Ireland. Regrettably, what W.G. Strickland, in his *Dictionary of Irish Artists*, had to say in 1913, still applies:

> From the time of its foundation to the present day the Academy has struggled against adverse circumstances, partly from the neglect and apathy of the public and partly from

the difficulty which was found in filling the ranks of the Academicians with artists who could paint. The history of art in Ireland – as can be seen from the account of artists given in the foregoing pages – shows that young artists of talent and ambition would not remain where there was no outlet for showing their powers, but emigrated to London.

Fortunately, during the first half of the nineteenth century, there were many artists who did not emigrate. But not all of them became good members of the RHA. Some, like James *Ills 82–3* Arthur O'Connor, fixed their sights neither on London nor Dublin. And the phenomenon which at first permitted, and then gradually encouraged, these painters was the rise of landscape painting.

During the eighteenth century in Ireland landscape painting, with the exception of Barret and one or two like him, had been largely an extension of portrait painting, a question of the land-owner having himself, his wife, his family, his horse, his favourite dog, his house and his land painted for him, usually though not always in that order of preference, and often by a variety of artists. 'Pure landscape' was an arcadian myth, needing either a temple or bathing nymphs to save it from dullness. It was only with the growing interest in the idea of the 'picturesque' that a change began to take place, and scenery to assume importance not only for its actual beauty, but also for the inspiration by which the scenery, through the artist, could lead to a picture which was an 'event' recording a moment in time, rather than being just a topographical record. This change, the importance of which is very great, liberated the artist from the confines of place. His first consideration ceased to be the accurate portrayal of a piece of country and became the sympathetic creation of a work of art. The two are not, of course, mutually exclusive. It is solely a question of priorities. *Ill. 82* But when James Arthur O'Connor painted *The Poachers* towards the end of his career, one in which he had suffered almost continual neglect, he demonstrated once again his life-

82 JAMES ARTHUR O'CONNOR *The Poachers*

long belief in a kind of landscape that liberated the painter from
the limited confines of topographical patronage, whether in
oils, watercolours or engravings, and gave him the right to
paint pictures in which the mood and atmosphere, the time of
day and the season of the year, the originality of composition
and the communication of an event or moment in time mattered
more than the locality and who owned it.

James Arthur O'Connor (1792–1841) was the son of an   *Ills 82–3*
engraver and print-seller and is said to have received lessons in
painting from William Sadler, who was some ten years his
senior. O'Connor's development as a painter was slow. His
early landscapes have poor tonal balance, and are dark without
having any of the luminous quality of the later paintings of
gorges and glens to compensate. The influence of Sadler,   *Ill. 85*

fortunately, was slight, and it is probable that O'Connor taught himself, a great deal of the time with reference to the prints which his father sold. Among these he must have seen many of the engravings of seventeenth-century Dutch landscape, and if any influence is paramount in his work it is that of Hobbema and his contemporaries. It can be seen both in his figures and in his composition, and on occasions his trees seem to derive directly from the Dutch Master, after whom O'Connor was nicknamed 'the Irish Hobbema'. After returning from Bristol, O'Connor worked in Dublin, but without much success, and it was only in 1818 that he got his first and only important commission when he was asked by the Marquess of Sligo to visit Westport and paint landscapes there. He spent a year and a half at Westport House and on other estates in the west of Ireland, and some of his most impressive paintings were done at this *Ill. 83* time: large views of Westport, Clew Bay, Mount Browne, Finlough, and the lakes and mountains of Connemara. Impressive as they are, however, they are fundamentally alien to O'Connor's nature. They are commissioned works, formal and rather stilted, composed to fit in a house or 'view' for the Marquess or some other patron, and lacking the warm intimacy in which O'Connor's own wayward choice of subject and approach would have resulted. The importance of these works in his development, on the other hand, is very considerable. They gave O'Connor the chance to develop his technical range, to experiment with different types of landscape, to work free from financial worry and in the process to discover the sort of landscape painting he really wanted to do. He returned to Dublin for a year or so, married, and in about 1821 went to London. For the last twenty years of his life he travelled a great deal, but continued to send pictures to the Royal Academy, the British Institution and the Society of British Artists, as well as the RHA in 1836 and 1840. He visited Brussels in 1826, and in 1832-3 he was on an extensive tour through Paris and into Germany, painting a number of landscapes along the Rhine. He seems to have visited Ireland at least twice during the 1830s,

83 JAMES ARTHUR O'CONNOR *View of Westport House*

but was living in London, still not able to sell much of his work, and suffering in the last years from weak sight and ill-health.

O'Connor was a careful and meticulous painter. He worked often from small and carefully drawn sketches in sepia pen and wash, and occasionally in watercolour, and both the British Museum and the National Gallery of Ireland have small collections of these, the former's relating to Sligo and Germany, the latter's to London and Kent shortly after O'Connor's arrival there. His best paintings have a great sense of 'moment' about them, with a well-drawn shepherd or labourer coming home through the stillness of a summer's day, a boy fishing beside a stream or in a glen, or the more stormy aspect, perhaps without figures at all, of such 'tourist attractions' as the Devil's Glen or the Glen of the Dargle. O'Connor's tone and colour are balanced, fresh and vivid. His composition is good, and his little figures in their red waistcoats, which are almost a signature in his paintings, are well placed and well drawn.

While O'Connor may be regarded as the father of modern landscape painting in Ireland, he had few followers or imitators just as he had few buyers or patrons. At the same time a group of watercolourists and landscape artists did emerge who achieved in their work the same freeing of their art from the restrictions *Ill. 84* of the late eighteenth century. One was George Chinnery (1774–1852). He was not Irish, but lived and worked in Dublin from about 1795 to 1802, and was influential among Irish painters of the period. He did portraits, miniatures and landscapes in watercolour, the latter of which show the influence of Rowlandson. He also married while in Dublin, and had two children, but deserted his family and set out for the Far East where he spent the rest of his life, partly doing formal portraits but for the most part engaged in prolific graphic work of a very high standard. Chinnery was a first-class draughtsman and graphic journalist, and the many thousands of his pencil and pen drawings in the Victoria and Albert Museum and other public and private collections have a uniquely vivid and *Ill. 85* immediate quality. William Sadler (1782–1839) taught O'Connor, though not for long, and was easily outstripped by

84 GEORGE CHINNERY *Coastal Scene near Dublin*

85 WILLIAM SADLER *King's Bridge and Kilmainham Gate, Dublin*

the younger man in every respect. At the same time Sadler had a lively and attractive style, with a good sense of movement in his figures. Some of his best paintings are his most simple rural views, but he worked fast and easily, and turned his hand to a wide range of subjects, including the portrayal of buildings, historic events and large views of towns and cities.

One other lone figure of this period was Gaspare Gabrielli *Ill. 86* (*fl.* 1805–30), an Italian decorative artist brought to Ireland in 1805 by Lord Cloncurry and employed in the decorating of Lyons House in County Kildare. He married Lady Cloncurry's maid and settled in Dublin, and during the period 1809–14 he exhibited over sixty Irish landscapes, very few of which seem to have survived. Many of them were in gouache, his favourite medium, but his oils, too, are very fine, and he was thought better than T. S. Roberts in his day, an opinion supported by his Roman landscapes in Glasgow, the Guildhall collection and in private hands.

The landscape artists in watercolour during the first half of the nineteenth century were led by John Henry Campbell *Ill. 87*

117

86 GASPARE GABRIELLI *Irish Landscape*

(1757–1828), a much under-rated artist, poorly represented in the principal public collections by faded and damaged drawings, and whose landscapes in oil, some of them very competent, are virtually unknown. He was a rather formal artist in his composition, carefully constructing a 'frame' of foreground trees and foliage for his main subject. But for a watercolourist working as early as he did, his washes are beautifully clear, fresh and vivid, his technique open and free, and his sense of *Ill. 87* light and perspective impeccable. His view of Dublin Bay and Harbour from Dundrum is one of a series done in 1804, the period of his finest work. Campbell was influenced by Sandby, and did some copies of his watercolours. He exhibited regularly in Dublin, but not with many works, and it would seem, from the number of his watercolours which come up at country auctions in large houses, that Campbell travelled round Ireland giving lessons in art to the families of the landed gentry.

Campbell's daughter, Cecilia Margaret Campbell (1791–1857), was one of Ireland's first women artists, and an able painter both in watercolour and oil. Her watercolours are not

87 JOHN HENRY CAMPBELL *View of Dublin Bay*

88 HENRY O'NEILL *The River Blackwater near Fermoy*

up to the same standard as those of her father, tending to be rather flat, and with weakly drawn figures, but her washes are good, and she has a spirited and individual way with trees and foliage. She married George Nairn (1799–1850), a competent *Ill. 88* and distinctive painter of animal portraits. Henry O'Neill (1798–1880) was a landscape artist of considerable power who was trained in the Dublin Society schools, probably under Henry Brocas, and then taught drawing. Some of his best landscapes were published as coloured aquatints in the 1830s, and he also painted some extensive canvases in oil. In later life O'Neill became involved in politics and archaeology, and his painting suffered, falling much below the early high standard. His associate in some of the publishing ventures of the 1830s, *Ill. 89* Andrew Nicholl (1804–86), was a northern artist, born in Belfast, and active as a landscape artist in northern Ireland, England and Dublin. He taught painting in Ceylon for a time but returned to London, then to Dublin and Belfast. He is a good watercolourist, quite close in style to Petrie and O'Neill, and his handling of open landscapes and coastal scenes, as well as mountains and trees, is highly competent.

89 ANDREW NICHOLL *Mourne Mountains from the Road near Castlewellan*

90 MICHAEL ANGELO HAYES *Sackville Street, Dublin*

Edward Hayes (1797–1864) painted both portraits and landscapes in watercolour. His portraits are close in style to the enlarged miniatures of Chinnery and the early, full-length portrait drawings by Daniel Maclise. His landscapes tend to be weak in perspective and loose in composition. George Grattan (1787–1819) started out by painting rather charming rustic scenes, but graduated to historical painting for which he was not as well equipped. *A Village Merrymaking* in the National Gallery of Ireland is a lively if rather clumsy example of his work. George Holmes was another artist active in Dublin at the turn of the century, and numerous views done by him were engraved. William Henry Brooke (1772–1860) was the son of an Irish historical painter of the eighteenth century, and did some Irish landscapes which were published in various periodicals and books.

Ill. 84
Ill. 105

Michael Angelo Hayes (1820–77) was an estimable artist whose watercolours are well drawn, with good perspective and composition. He enjoyed drawing and painting horses, and was responsible for the Bianconi 'Car-Travelling' prints, as well as a number of other engraved works.

Ill. 90

91 SAMUEL FREDERICK BROCAS *Post Office and Sackville Street, Dublin*

During the whole of the first half of the nineteenth century the teaching of landscape painting in the Dublin Society schools was in the hands of the Brocases, Henry Senior and Junior, and they came from a family of artists, of whom the best known *Ill. 91* was Samuel Frederick Brocas (1792–1847). His views of Dublin were etched by his brother, Henry Junior (1798–1873) and published in 1820. They are among the most spirited views of Dublin, full of life and activity, although in the drawing and the engraving much inferior to Malton's work. The father, Henry Brocas Senior (1762–1837), was a better and far more prolific engraver than his son, and an artist of some merit in both watercolour and oils. The Victoria and Albert Museum has an interesting sketchbook of drawings by William Brocas (1794–1868), but the National Gallery of Ireland has re-attributed a painting of Bray Head formerly ascribed to him to his brother, Samuel Frederick.

Ill. 92 George Petrie (1790–1866) followed a career not unlike that of Henry O'Neill, although rather more distinguished. His early watercolours are fine, soft landscapes with broad washes and an excellent sense of light and distance. But his graphic ability was noticed by various publishers, and he was engaged

122

in a number of ventures as a book illustrator. This curtailed his scope and narrowed his vision. It also led him into dedicated and extremely valuable work as an archaeologist, a member of the Royal Irish Academy, and a member of the Royal Hibernian Academy, of which he became librarian and eventually President. He was involved in the Ordnance Survey of Ireland, and also did much research into Irish music. His watercolour painting suffered as a result of all this, and his early work is generally considered to be his best.

George Petrie was preceded in the post of President of the RHA by two fine portrait painters, William Cuming (1769–1852) and Martin Cregan (1788–1870). Cregan was the first and only pupil of Martin Archer Shee, and a friend of Constable *Ill. 97* and Landseer. He returned to Dublin in 1822 and worked successfully in the city for the rest of his life. His portraits are lively, sensitive and attractive, and he was particularly good at

92 GEORGE PETRIE *Gougane Barra*

painting pretty women. Cuming was also highly thought of for his portraits of women, and was a leading artist in Dublin for the first thirty years of the century.

Other painters of the period working in Dublin include the Mulvaneys: Thomas James (1779–1845), John George (1766–1838) and George Francis (1809–69), son of T.J. and the best of the three, although his fame rests primarily on his work in getting a National Gallery established and his management of it as its first director. Joseph Patrick Haverty (1794–1864) was a Galway painter who did much of his work in Limerick, as well as exhibiting in Dublin and London. Nicholas Joseph Crowley (1819–57) painted portraits in Dublin, but concentrated *Ill. 93* his energies on Belfast. His self-portrait is in the Ulster Museum there. The work of Bernard Mulrenin also belongs to this period.

Ill. 67 The leading miniaturist after Horace Hone, who continued working until 1822, was John Comerford (1770–1832). He was an energetic and successful artist, and many of his miniatures

93 NICHOLAS J. CROWLEY
Self-portrait

94 JOHN HENRY FOLEY
Oliver Goldsmith

124

and small drawings are excellent. He stood aloof from the groups of artists in Ireland, and like James Barry he despised academies for artists. Strickland quotes him as saying, 'Those who encourage young men to become artists were doing a real and substantial injury to society; they were destroying very excellent carpenters, smiths and house-painters, and creating a class of unfortunates who never would be capable of doing any good for either themselves or others,' and his sentiments have frequently been repeated, often by the best of painters. Charles Robertson (1760–1821) was another excellent miniaturist, and he trained his daughter, Clementina (1795–1853), in the same art.

It is of interest that no less than three of the eight sculptors employed on the Albert Memorial were Irish, the most important being John Henry Foley (1818–74), who was responsible for the bronze statue of Prince Albert and for the group representing 'Asia'. Foley is the most important sculptor Ireland has ever produced. His work ranges from the relatively intimate Oliver Goldsmith outside Trinity College to the *Ill. 94* monumental O'Connell memorial in O'Connell Street. His equestrian statue of Viscount Hardinge is a superb epitome of the Victorian age in England, with its ideals of imperial responsibility, and Foley's response to this atmosphere was a conscientious and, at times, inspired one. Patrick MacDowell (1799–1870) was a Belfast sculptor, and responsible for the 'Europe' group on the memorial, as well as many statues and busts in Belfast, Dublin and London. John Lawlor (1820–1901) and Samuel Ferris Lynn (1834–76) also worked with Foley on the Albert Memorial. John Edward Carew (1782–1868) was another important Irish sculptor of the period who worked mostly in England. Others, whose names only can be given, include Christopher Moore (1790–1863), John Hogan (1800–58), Peter Turnerelli (1774–1839), Joseph Watkins (1838–71), the Gahagans, Laurence (1756–1817) and Sebastien (1800–35), Thomas Kirk (1781–1845) and finally Joseph Robinson Kirk (1821–94).

The last and perhaps the most interesting group of artists of this period are those who, like Francis Danby, left Ireland to *Ills 95–6* make their reputations in London. Francis Danby (1793–1861) painted both in watercolour and oils. His watercolours are finely drawn pictures, with good if sometimes rather lush vegetation, somewhat in the style of John Martin, and an *Ill. 95* excellent handling of light and shade. His *Temple of Flora* has all Danby's excellence of technique in watercolour, but carries his work on into the realm of mythology, a direction which his oil paintings followed with much greater persistence, but with far less ability. In most of his oils Danby seems to be attempting 'sublime' subjects. Not only are these often bathetic, *The Opening of the Sixth Seal* in the National Gallery of Ireland being a fair example, they are also painted in harsh and lurid colours which have suffered with age. Danby's fascination with sunset has been his undoing in many pictures, even the straightforward *Ill. 96* seascapes. Occasionally, as in *Liensford Lake, Norway* in the Victoria and Albert Museum, good paintings have survived. His watercolours, however, are quite a different matter. In them he kept generally to landscapes without mythological or historical attributes, and while he favoured strong contrasts of light and shade, stormy weather and clear skies combined in the same paintings, he kept well within the realm of nature. Martin Hardie, in his *Water-Colour Painting in Britain*, describes Danby as one of the most interesting and gifted artists of the Romantic period, and in watercolours this is very true, both in the artist's technique and his vision.

Ill. 97 Sir Martin Archer Shee (1769–1850) had already been painting in London for twenty-five years when O'Connor, Petrie and Danby paid their brief visit, and after much struggling and difficulty had achieved an important position as a portrait painter. He came originally from Dublin, although his family had roots in Kilkenny and Mayo, and after training in art at the Dublin Society schools he established himself in the city as a portrait painter. Gilbert Stuart advised him to go to London, which he did. He was helped by another Irish artist, Alexander

95, 96 FRANCIS DANBY *The Temple of Flora* and *Liensford Lake, Norway*

97 SIR MARTIN ARCHER SHEE
Self-portrait

Pope (1763–1835) and by Edmund Burke, and by 1800 was a
well-established London portrait painter. By the time he was
made President of the Royal Academy after Lawrence's death
in 1830, Shee had a considerable reputation as a writer as well
as an artist.

Ill. 97   Shee's earliest work is often regarded as his best, and certainly
the simple directness of the self-portrait has a quite different
and rather more immediate appeal than the splendid and
flamboyant portrait of King William IV. The first dates from
1794, the second from the 1830s. Yet the second, and the many
others painted during the artist's maturity, have many of the
best qualities of drama and portent which Shee understood so
well and presented with vigour and technical excellence. His
portrait of Thomas Moore in the National Gallery of Ireland is
a sensitive study somewhere between the self-portrait and the
King William.

Richard Rothwell (1800–68) was an artist who, like Barret,
lacked the self-confidence and strength of character to with-
stand the bad advice of artists who wish to persuade others to
follow their style, however inappropriate. He would have been
an excellent portrait painter, working much in the style of

128

98 RICHARD ROTHWELL
A Smiling Child

Lawrence, whose pupil he was, as his *A Smiling Child* shows. *Ill. 98*
But he felt ignorant about the great painters of the past, decided
that he should try to emulate them, and was persuaded by
B. R. Haydon to undertake historical art. *Callisto*, in the National
Gallery of Ireland, is a good example of how mistaken this
decision was. Rothwell's career became a fragmented and
psychologically rather tortured one, and the fact that he
regarded *Callisto* as his finest work is indicative of the distortion
of his vision. His portrait of Mary Shelley in the National
Portrait Gallery is a fine and sympathetic work, and so are those
of Matthew Kendrick and Gerald Griffin in the National
Gallery of Ireland. Rothwell died in Rome, and was buried
beside Keats.

Amelia Curran (1775–1847), the eldest daughter of John
Philpot Curran, deserves mention for one striking portrait, that
of Percy Bysshe Shelley in the National Portrait Gallery. It is an
unfinished work, but for an amateur artist it is remarkably
sympathetic.

Two highly accomplished miniaturists worked in London *Ills 99, 100*
at this time, Samuel Lover (1797–1868) and Adam Buck (1759–
1833). Buck came from Cork, and worked there until his move

99 ADAM BUCK
'*Mama don't make me
beg in vain,/Pray read
that pretty book again*'

to London in 1795. Many of his miniatures are full-length, either standing or seated, and there is a fine self-portrait in the Courtauld Institute, as well as an excellent set of profiles and portraits of two girls, one seated and one standing, signed and dated 1800. His posing in these pictures is somewhat rigid. In *Ill. 99* his lifetime he became better known, however, for his 'fancy subjects', many of which were engraved. These have a certain innocent charm, though their aesthetic relevance is somewhat questionable.

Samuel Lover's career was rather more varied than Buck's, but he was not so good an artist. His miniatures are close in style, and he also did small full-lengths, but these tend to be larger and more elaborate, the heads carefully painted, the rest *Ill. 100* sketched in. His self-portrait in the National Gallery of Ireland is a good example of his work. He was also a novelist and musician, and towards the end of his life earned considerable sums of money giving what he called 'Irish Evenings', made up of his own compositions.

130

The last two artists to be considered in this chapter are probably the two Irish painters who made the biggest impact on English art during the first half of the nineteenth century, Daniel Maclise (1806–70) and William Mulready (1786–1863). Both are under-rated painters. Mulready started painting very early, and had already received lessons from John Graham, Baynes and Banks the sculptor before going to the Royal Academy school at the age of fourteen. He came originally from Ennis, County Clare. He was a meticulous painter, and many slight, often tiny, preparatory sketches for details in his paintings exist. He once told Samuel Palmer that 'all the best artists had begun with what is called niggling.' And it even went so far that he would produce full-size watercolour sketches of his paintings before actually tackling his canvases. But he was usually able to offset the danger of laboured appearances in his work by the atmosphere of action and suspense which his own style of genre painting led him to. In his *Bathers Surprised*, the pink-fleshed and voluptuous nudes are presented in somewhat puritanical environment by the story which the picture tells, a story which is going on *behind* the central figure, as if they were a backcloth, which in fact they are. There is a similar, but rather more natural painting in the same style in the Municipal

Ills 104–6
Ills 101–3

Ill. 102

100 SAMUEL LOVER *Self-portrait*

101 WILLIAM MULREADY *Self-portrait*

Gallery of Modern Art in Dublin, and others elsewhere, as well as a fine preliminary drawing of four nude girls bathing in Edinburgh. Perhaps Mulready felt he had to dress his nudes in genre clothing. Certainly he was never as brazen as William Etty.

Ill. 103　Mulready's best work was in the straightforward 'telling of a story'. *The Last In* is an excellent example of this, and one of Mulready's most charming pictures. 'Charm' and 'delight' are words that one applies frequently to his art. He paints with great warmth and sympathy, achieves excellent tension, excitement and drama, and yet rarely steps beyond the most ordinary of events, mostly concerned with children, family, animals and simple domestic squabbles, dramas and frustration. A third area in which Mulready was active was landscape, in which he produced a number of good but unpretentious works. He also painted some portraits, among them a very slight but excellent picture of his father in the National Gallery of Ireland, and a good though unfinished self-portrait.

Ills 104–6　Daniel Maclise started out as a portrait artist, drawing and painting in watercolour small cameo portraits, some of which

102 WILLIAM MULREADY
Bathers Surprised

103 WILLIAM MULREADY
(right above) *The Last In*

104 DANIEL MACLISE
A Winter Night's Tale

are in the British Museum, signed with an early version of his name, McClise. He was born in Cork, almost certainly in 1806 although the date is disputed. His early work was done there, and he was 'discovered' by Walter Scott when he did a rather successful sketch of the writer, a version of which is also in the British Museum. On Scott's advice he went to London and studied at the RA schools. He still continued portrait painting, and produced many of his literary friends, both in small drawings which appeared in *Frazer's Magazine* under his pseudonym, 'Alfred Croquis', and in oils, one of the best being

Ill. 105 of his lifelong friend, Charles Dickens.

But Maclise was attracted by narrative painting; his friendship with writers and actors gave a somewhat literary bias to this interest, and led him to paint many Shakespearean subjects, one of the first being *Malvolio affecting the Count*, which was his first picture submitted to the RA in 1829. Throughout the 1830s and 1840s he painted large canvases with immense technical skill and attention to detail, and managed at the same time to maintain unity and balance in subject, colour and composition. The best of these narrative pictures are those which are most

105 DANIEL MACLISE *Portrait of Charles Dickens*

106 DANIEL MACLISE *The Marriage of Princess Aoife and Strongbow*

intimate, however, and some of them are superb paintings, rich and warm in colour and tone, intense in statement and beautifully composed. Among them is one in the Walker Art Gallery in Liverpool, *Madeline after Prayer* and *A Winter Night's Tale* in the Manchester City Art Galleries. Some of Maclise's straightforward subject pictures, such as *The Falconer* in the Municipal Gallery in Cork, are also fine works.

Ill. 104

In the late 1850s Maclise was engaged on the decorations for the new Houses of Parliament, and in 1859 he completed his wall painting of *Wellington meeting Blucher*. Five years later he finished his *Death of Nelson*, but although he had arranged to do others for the building he declined. *The Marriage of Princess Aoife and Strongbow* was to have been done for Westminster as well, but was not included in the scheme. The canvas picture, which is on the same massive scale, is probably his largest oil painting. He has been much maligned, both on account of technique and inspiration, and he has suffered from countless appearances in school textbooks. He is an important artist, and an influential one, and in his best pictures a sympathetic and highly effective creator of atmosphere and tension.

Ill. 106

135

The Celtic revival

In his poem 'The Municipal Gallery Revisited', William Butler Yeats attempts to draw together the threads of the past as they appear to him in the paintings, and as they relate to the ideals of J.M. Synge, Lady Gregory and himself. What he wrote of Mancini's portrait of Augusta Gregory might well have been the poet's comment on the whole era and its generation of Irish men and women:

> But where is the brush that could show anything
> Of all that pride and that humility?
> And I am in despair that time may bring
> Approved patterns of women or of men
> But not that selfsame excellence again.

Yeat's appeal as a poet lies to a great extent in his sense of *le temps perdu*, and his ability to recapture and synthesize the multiple threads of the past. He draws together John Butler Yeats, John Lavery, Hugh Lane, even Sargent, Mancini, Shannon, and he evokes a period out of the past. But how personal is it, and how reliable? The poet celebrates 1916. But what notion had he of its coming? To what extent can the art of a period, in this instance from the Famine to the Rising, have more than accidental relevance to history as it pursues its highly individual route into posterity or oblivion?

Ills 127–9
Ill. 125

The only certain thing about Irish art in the period from 1850 to 1916 (an arbitrary date, it must be admitted, but a convenient one), is its diverse and fragmented nature. No simple pattern emerges. The only names to dominate are the highly individual ones of Nathaniel Hone, Roderic O'Conor, Walter Osborne, John Butler Yeats, Sir William Orpen and Sir John Lavery. There is added diversity of media, with the

Ills 107–8
Ills 109–11
Ills 123–5

important development of Irish stained glass. But beyond the loosely corporate activity of groups of painters, such as those working in Antwerp, there is little or no real unity, a situation to be explained by the fact that the most important styles of painting pursued – landscape, genre and historical painting – were basically solitary.

The greatest Irish landscape painter of the period, Nathaniel Hone (1831–1917), epitomizes this situation. He was a descendant of Berkeley Hone, brother of the eighteenth-century portrait painter, but began life as an engineer, taking up painting only when he was twenty-two, and going to study it in Paris under Adolphe Yvon, and later under Thomas Couture. He then moved to Barbizon, and worked there in close contact with Jean-François Millet and Henri Harpignies, painting landscapes exclusively, and, apart from visits to the Mediterranean, remaining in that famous village for close to twenty years. In about 1875 he returned to Ireland, and spent the rest of his life in

Ills 107–8

107 NATHANIEL HONE *Pastures at Malahide*

108 NATHANIEL HONE *Off Lowestoft*

north County Dublin, painting and farming. He did not really need to sell his work in order to live, and apart from his regular submissions to the annual exhibition of the RHA, of which he became a member in 1880, Hone did not show widely, tending to remain aloof and indifferent towards critics and other painters who were not his friends. He accepted the RHA Professorship of Painting in 1894 which he held until his death.

While Hone's approach to landscape is distinguished by its Barbizon traits, his application of them to his Irish environment is assured, sympathetic and profound. His horizon-line is generally low, giving him adequate space for his magnificently painted skies and for the immensely subtle play of light and colour which is so essential a part of Irish landscape. *Pastures at* *Ill. 107* *Malahide* is Hone at his best. His composition, in which the sky is dominant, is simple and powerful. His colour, while restrained, is fresh and vital. And in spite of the peaceful and unified tranquillity of the subject, the painting has enormous strength and vigour.

It was Thomas Bodkin's opinion, in his *Four Irish Landscape Painters*, published three years after Hone's death, that less than

138

a hundred of Hone's oil paintings were in private collections. The rest, some 550 oils and nearly 900 watercolours and drawings, were left to the National Gallery of Ireland, where the greater part of them are stored away. The majority will never be shown, and Hone will never be 'marketed', a fate which will always limit appreciation to a small number of admirers, and make possession an eternally circumscribed privilege.

Hone also painted many seascapes, not only near his home, in the west of Ireland, but also in Britain and abroad. They again reveal his simple but assured mastery of composition, light and colour. His watercolours are constant annotations of light and shade, and of the ever-changing patterns of colour in landscape. They are mostly jottings, of the sort Constable took, but when Hone does become expansive his washes and colours are excellent.

In Roderick O'Conor (1861–1940), France attracted another Irish painter of great range and distinction, who went there in his early twenties and never came back. O'Conor's origins are obscure, and his life, to say the least, that of a recluse. He hated art dealers, and rarely exhibited his pictures or sold them. In 1906 he gave his *A Young Breton Girl* to the new Municipal *Ill. 109* Gallery of Modern Art in Dublin, but in general, work left his studio only to private buyers, among them Somerset Maugham, who had several of his works, which O'Conor parted with somewhat ungraciously. O'Conor was a friend of Gauguin, and lived and worked at Pont-Aven, where some of his finest landscapes were painted. Gauguin wanted him to go to the South Seas, but O'Conor declined. He had discovered, in the wild and isolated landscape of Brittany, a totally absorbing subject for his art, and he was lucky enough to be able to settle for that. In the 1920s the English painter, Matthew Smith, worked with O'Conor for a time, and was, by his own admission, influenced more by him than by any other artist.

There are three not very distinct periods in O'Conor's work. The first is the most impressionist, from about 1889 to 1900, when O'Conor was painting strongly under van Gogh's

109 RODERICK O'CONOR
A Young Breton Girl

110 RODERICK O'CONOR
Self-portrait

111 RODERICK O'CONOR *Field of Corn, Pont-Aven*

influence, though whether he knew van Gogh is not clear. These early pictures employ a stripy technique, not unlike van Gogh's, with quite heavy paint, but relatively subdued colours. From 1900 to 1910 is the artist's best period. His colours become rich, strong and beautifully balanced, and a highly distinctive palette emerges in these canvases. After 1910 his work becomes more diverse, his style ranges more widely, possibly with a certain loss of intensity.

His self-portrait reveals something of O'Conor's introspective and anti-social nature, as well as his very French appearance, his sallow complexion, dark hair and drooping moustache. His wife was also an artist.

A group of Irish artists also worked in Belgium, and this 'Antwerp School' of the 1880s was led by Walter Frederick *Ills 112–14* Osborne (1859–1903), the son of William Osborne (1823–1901), himself a good artist who painted mainly animals and hunting scenes. The younger Osborne was trained by the RHA and was a frequent prize-winner. He studied in Antwerp under Verlat in 1882–3, and after his return he spent ten years travelling and painting landscapes in England, Spain, Brittany and Holland, as well as urban scenes. His view of the promenade in Hastings is a finely composed picture, with the excellent impression of golden light falling on the buildings in the background, and the finely grouped foreground figures.

His early landscapes, such as *Apple Garden at Quimperlé* in the National Gallery of Ireland, have a wonderful, timeless innocence about them, and his painting of children, from the very beginning, was accomplished. This is particularly apparent in his poignant Dublin street scenes, in which he concentrated on the forlorn and hopeless poverty of the areas around St Patrick's Cathedral, the Coombe and the various city markets. There is splendid atmosphere in *Saint Patrick's Close, Dublin.* *Ill. 114* The greyness, the grime, the smell, the squalor, are almost palpable, and the foreground figure of the boy with his whistle, and then another child, and yet another, provide a subtle entry into the damp, bleak street, with its stalls and derelict houses.

112 WALTER OSBORNE *Nathaniel Hone*

113 WALTER OSBORNE *Hastings*

These views belong to the late 1880s and 1890s. At this time
Osborne also took up portrait painting, and while much of the
work involved attracted him far less than did landscape, he was
good at it, and on occasion produced very fine likenesses,
among them his excellent portrait of Nathaniel Hone. Osborne   *Ill. 112*
produced a number of watercolours, although his technique
was somewhat muddy. His general style was becoming a good
deal freer at the time of his early death from pneumonia.

Joseph Malachy Kavanagh (1856–1918) was a friend of   *Ill. 115*
Osborne and one of the artists who studied at Antwerp. He
seems to have been rather more precise and clear-cut in his
composition than Osborne, but he lacked the inspiration of his
friend's painting, and the majority of his works are rather
limited in range. He handled figures poorly, but his sense of
light was superb, and some of his best works are his simple
seashore pieces, with their low horizons and massed, sun-
drenched clouds, their pinks and golds reflected in wet sand.

114 WALTER OSBORNE
Saint Patrick's Close, Dublin

115 JOSEPH MALACHY KAVANAGH
Old Convent Gate, Dinan

Many of the Antwerp artists went on to Brittany to paint. Others in the group include Dermod O'Brien (1865–1945) who became President of the RHA in 1910. He painted many good, though rather low-key landscapes; Richard Thomas Moynan (1856–1906), a technically able painter who wandered off into rather indecisive genre pictures; Henry Allan (1865–1912), Nathaniel Hill and Frank O'Meara.

A more diverse group of landscape painters were working in Ireland at a slightly earlier period, including three excellent *Ills 116–17* painters of seascapes, John Faulkner (*fl.* 1852–87), Edwin Hayes (1820–1904) and George Mounsey Wheatley Atkinson (1806–84). Faulkner's watercolours are usually quite large and spirited in treatment, often showing stormy seas, as in his *Off Cape* *Ill. 116* *Clear, Co. Cork.* He also painted in oils, but seems to have preferred watercolour. He painted in the United States for a while, and in London; but his life was somewhat obscure, and *Ill. 117* not many of his works are known. Edwin Hayes studied in the Dublin Society's schools, and then went to sea, though always with the determination of becoming a marine painter. He worked in Dublin until 1852, and then went to London. His

116 JOHN FAULKNER *Off Cape Clear, Co. Cork*

117 EDWIN HAYES *Entrance to Cardiff*

sea paintings have great realism and accuracy. Atkinson was a
Cork artist, self-taught, and tending to paint 'portraits' of ships
which are often sought after more for their subject than their
creator. J. Glen Wilson, the Belfast artist, also painted good
marine pictures.

William Davis (1812–73) is an important Irish landscape
artist who was born and trained in Dublin, and began by
working in the city as a portrait painter. Fortunately he was
unsuccessful, and turned to landscape painting, producing his
fine *Junction of the Liffey and Rye, near Leixlip* before leaving
Dublin to live and work in Liverpool. There his landscape
technique developed considerably, and he acquired a highly
individual approach to colour and detail, very rich and rather
strange in atmosphere and feeling, and close to the landscape
style adopted by some of the Pre-Raphaelite landscape artists.

Ill. 118

145

118 WILLIAM DAVIS *Junction of the Liffey and Rye, Near Leixlip*

There is great mood in his painting, much of which derives from his almost surrealist treatment of some of the figures.

Thomas Bridgford (1812–78) was an artist whose style was quite close to that of Davis. He painted genre pictures and portraits rather than landscapes. Augustus Nicholas Burke (1838–91) painted good though less individual landscapes than Davis, some of them in Brittany. William Howis (1804–82) painted landscapes in the style of James Arthur O'Connor, and even did a number of good copies of O'Connor's work, many of which were sold as the work of the earlier artist. John O'Connor (1830–89) was initially a theatre call-boy, but turned to scene painting and landscapes, at which he became highly accomplished, working throughout the British Isles.

Among landscape painters in watercolour were William Craig (1829–75); James Mahony (1810–79), who painted fine and extensive scenes in Dublin, some of them interiors; Bartholomew Colles Watkins (1833–91), who was primarily a painter in oils, but whose watercolours tend to be better and

Ills 82–3

146

more sensitive; and Alexander Williams (d. 1930), who also painted in both oil and watercolour. Percy French (1854–1920) started out from Trinity College, Dublin, as an engineer, but seems, not unlike Samuel Lover, to have spent a delightful lifetime composing, singing and painting watercolours. Another writer who painted with some distinction in watercolour was Edith Œ. Somerville (1858–1949).

Jeremiah Hodges Mulcahy (d. 1889) was a Limerick painter whose work is detailed and meticulous, almost eighteenth century in style. His composition was occasionally weak and stilted, but his *Curragh Chase* in the National Gallery of Ireland is a good example of his work. Alfred Elmore (1815–81) was a Cork painter, trained in London and Paris, and became a successful artist of genre pictures.

Sir Frederick William Burton (1816–1900) was a very *Ill. 119* accomplished watercolourist and draughtsman whose best work was probably in portraiture. His *The Aran Fisherman's Drowned Child*, in the National Gallery of Ireland, is a melodramatic but well-drawn picture. Michael G. Brennan (1839–71) was an Irish painter who worked almost all his life in Capri. Before settling there, however, he drew cartoons for a London journal called *Fun*, and was for a time the rival of another Irish

119 SIR FREDERICK WILLIAM BURTON
George Eliot

120 RICHARD DOYLE
Design for a Fairy Tale

Ill. 120 artist, Richard Doyle (1824–83) who created the old cover of
Punch as well as doing the illustrations for many books. His
father, John Doyle, was a political cartoonist; his brother,
Henry Edward Doyle, was a religious artist and Director of
the National Gallery of Ireland after Mulvaney; and two other
brothers, Charles (1832–93) and James William Edmund (1822–
92) were landscape painters in watercolour. Matthew James
Lawless (1837–64) was a brilliant but short-lived artist in oil
and watercolour who contributed many illustrations to books
and journals, and painted some excellent genre pictures
Ill. 122 including the fine *Sick Call*. Erskine Nicol (1825–1904) was not
Irish, but painted a number of subject and narrative pictures on
Ill. 121 Irish themes, including *Donnybrook Fair* and *The Emigrants*,
both in the Tate Gallery. His work is dramatic and well painted,

148

121 ERSKINE NICOL
The Emigrants

122 MATTHEW J. LAWLESS
The Sick Call

if at times over-theatrical. Nicol was Scottish, and there is a very fine self-portrait drawing in the National Portrait Gallery of Scotland. Alfred Grey and his father Charles (1808–92) were both good landscape artists, the father painting portraits as well, and the son animals, for which he had a rare gift.

In portrait painting, at the semi-official level which the period required, the second half of the nineteenth century was dominated by Stephen Catterson Smith (1806–72) and his son, also named Stephen (1849–1912). The father came to Ireland from Yorkshire to complete some portrait commissions in Londonderry in 1839, subsequently moving to Dublin where he painted with great success for the rest of his life. He was President of the RHA for two periods during the 1860s. He was a stylish artist, bred in the tradition of Sir Thomas Lawrence, though far less flamboyant. His *Self-Portrait* is a good example of his sympathy for form, texture and character in portraiture.

When Catterson Smith Senior died, his practice was taken over by his son, who was equally industrious, though not so gifted. He lacked his father's sympathy for character, and perhaps made up for this with increasingly massive full-length portraits of eminent Irish men and women. For many years he was Secretary of the RHA.

The period ends with several notable artists who are as diverse in style and vision as the painters who began it. William Newenham Montague Orpen (1878–1931), from a well-to-do County Dublin family, studied art at the Metropolitan School before going on to the Slade, where he was a contemporary of Augustus John. His development is closely parallel to that of John. His early drawings and landscapes in oil are light, free, assured and wide-ranging. He was a prolific draughtsman, and a very good one. His nudes, particularly, are drawn with great strength and understanding, and his female portraits are often a good deal more sympatheric than those of men.

Ills 123–4

From 1917 to 1919 Orpen was an official war artist, and a considerable collection of his drawings in France belong to the Imperial War Museum, London. He was at this stage a portrait

123 SIR WILLIAM ORPEN *The Model*

painter of some reputation, and while at times his portraits are rather shallow, he was capable of excellent and sympathetic work, particularly in family and group portraits. His groups of the Vere Foster family and of his parents (in the National Gallery of Ireland) are good examples of this, as well as his *Homage to Manet* in the City of Manchester Art Gallery and *A Bloomsbury Family* which belongs in mood to the school of Conder, Sickert and Rothenstein, with whom Orpen had much in common.

Ill. 124

He delighted in self-portrait; straightforward as well as theatrical and fanciful examples of these abound, most of them vigorous and effective. He often included himself in portrait

124 SIR WILLIAM ORPEN *A Bloomsbury Family*

groups, reflected in small convex mirrors which are a frequent
prop in his paintings. In his portrait drawings his style is close
to Augustus John's, and one of the finest of these is a study of
George Moore in the National Portrait Gallery. He returned to
Ireland in the 1920s, and wrote a sad, bad, but revealing book
called *Stories of Old Ireland and Myself*, in which he regrets the
changes in taste and the exclusion of people like himself.

152

The reaction against Orpen, a natural enough phenomenon given the history of the period, was combined with an equally natural reaction among artists after the First World War against the man who had so completely dominated the art scene in Dublin from 1900 to 1914. His pre-eminence then was a technical one, based on his brilliant draughtsmanship, his range and versatility, his intense professionalism as a painter. And it was these qualities that influenced many younger artists, the best of them being James Sleator, who subsequently became President of the RHA, Leo Whelan (1892–1956), who was the principal painter of portraits in Dublin from 1930 to 1950, Lady Glenavy and Kathleen Fox.

The career of John Lavery (1856–1941) is similar to Orpen's. *Ill. 125* He was born in Belfast and trained at art school in Glasgow,

125 SIR JOHN LAVERY
Hazel Lavery

where he practised for a while before continuing his studies in London and Paris. He then returned to Scotland, and became one of the 'Glasgow School' of painters, rapidly building up a considerable reputation, particularly in the portrayal of women. Like Orpen he worked as an official war artist, and they were both knighted in 1918.

Sarah Purser (1849–1943) was a central figure in art in Dublin, and a good portrait painter, although some of her finest and most sensitive work was not strictly portraiture, for example, *Ill. 126* *An Irish Idyll* in the Ulster Museum, and *Le Petit Déjeuner*. Sarah Purser was also active in the growth and development of Irish stained glass at the turn of the century. Sarah Celia Harrison (d. 1941) was another woman painter of the period whose portraits are honest and straightforward likenesses close in style to those of Sarah Purser.

Sarah Purser's association with the stained glass movement in Ireland at the beginning of the twentieth century was prompted by Edward Martyn, and her studio, which she ran until her death at the age of ninety-four, was founded in 1903. It was called *An Túr Gloine* (The Tower of Glass). Sarah Purser herself designed stained glass, but the real creative impulse for the movement came from Harry Clarke (1889–1931) and Michael Healy (1873–1941). Clarke was a highly distinctive artist with great individuality of style and vision. His debt to Beardsley is clear, as well as his acute consciousness of the concern with form and colour which characterized art training in Britain in the 1890s. Yet he was independent enough in his vision to be able to take these forces and adapt them to his own medium of stained glass with just the right mixture of tradition and individual talent. Michael Healy was very different. His vision was essentially a simple one, unsophisticated, and dependent on environment and people for form and inspiration in his art. Irish churches and cathedrals throughout the country bear ample witness to the original craftsmanship of both men. They were also excellent draughtsmen, Clarke a highly polished book illustrator, Healy a relaxed and unpretentious

154

watercolourist whose particular subjects were Dublin figures and street scenes. The greatest stained glass artist of all, however, was probably Evie Hone, who is dealt with in the next chapter. *Ill. 146* Others associated with the movement were Wilhelmina Margaret Geddes (1888–1955), Ethel Mary Rhind (d. 1952) and a number of living artists, Catherine A. O'Brien, Patrick Pollen, Hubert V. McGoldrick, Richard King, David, Anne, and Terence Clarke, and William Dowling.

The most sensitive Irish portrait painter of this period, and the man who captured more of the atmosphere of the Irish revival in the vision and determination of the leaders of his own generation whom he painted, was John Butler Yeats (1839– *Ills 127–9* 1922). He started life as an architect, and it was only in 1867, two years after the birth of his elder son, that he took up painting, studying at Heatherleys Art School. It is probable that the early influences on the painter were essentially English, and his technique has much in common with that of George Frederick Watts, in his simpler pieces, and Alfred Stevens. W. B. Yeats

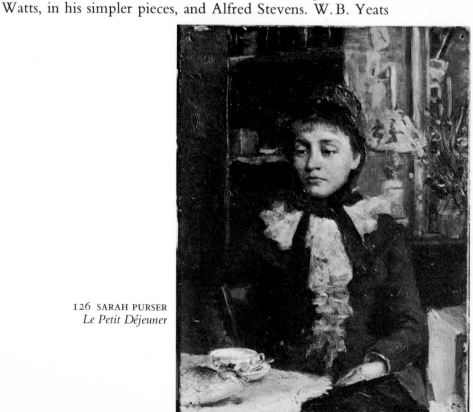

126 SARAH PURSER
Le Petit Déjeuner

127 JOHN BUTLER YEATS
Jack B. Yeats as a Boy

has referred to the influence of 'French art', but it seems clear that this was secondary to the prevailing atmosphere of Pre-Raphaelitism, although Yeats soon outstripped these early influences and adopted a direct and individual style which is already assured and deeply felt in his portrait of his son, *Ill. 127* Jack B. Yeats.

During the 1880s Yeats spent periods in London, at his home in Bedford Park, and also in Ireland, and it was not until 1902 that he left the Bedford Park settlement and moved to Ireland and finally to the United States. Bedford Park was a significant experiment in English art and architecture during the last twenty-five years of the nineteenth century, and the contribu-

128 JOHN BUTLER YEATS
William Butler Yeats

tion made by the elder Yeats was considerable. Unfortunately, one's knowledge of his work during this period is severely limited by the fact that the great majority of his paintings from the early years were destroyed by bombing during the Second World War.

His finest period of portrait painting commenced with his return to Dublin in 1902, and during the next few years he produced a series of great Irishmen as well as friends and relations. The immediate contact these works make is invariably through the eyes of the subject. Yeats was able to capture the essence of his sitter's character almost always in the eyes alone, and to add then the gesture, posture and facial bone structure

157

129 JOHN BUTLER YEATS
John Millington Synge

and detail in a loose and impressionistic style which rarely
faltered. The paintings of this period were accompanied by
Ill. 129 many drawings, some of them–for example, that of J.M.
Synge–quite superb. And Yeats continued to work with the
same assurance right up to his death, completing in 1920, for
example, the fine self-portrait in the National Portrait Gallery.
Ill. 128 It is perhaps appropriate to mention John Butler Yeats's
portrait of his other son, William Butler Yeats, done during the
Bedford Park phase, and one of the few portraits of the poet to
treat him as a man, and to invest him with human and lovable
qualities, youthful, thoughtful and sensitive.

158

Jack Yeats and the moderns

In 1897 Jack B. Yeats (1871–1957) was living in Devon. He *Ills 130–7* was twenty-six years old, and painting some of his most glorious watercolours. They are mostly scenes at fairs, race meetings, boxing booths and inns. Some of them are filled with bright, golden sunshine, such as *Waiting*, in which the colour, *Ill. 130* technique and composition reveal the artist's mastery of this particular medium. But not all of them are as light or sunny. In *His Thoughts to Himself* Yeats shows a rather more solemn aspect of his environment. The drawing is of an isolated figure on a bench in a bar, an empty glass beside him, his solemn face and clasped hands indicative of unsociable detachment. As a drawing it is not half as good as *Waiting*, which is among Yeats's finest watercolours. But as a picture it probably has more to tell us of Yeats's vision, and of his sense of responsibility as an artist, and in a strange way the title can be applied as easily to Yeats as to his subject.

Jack B. Yeats is something of an enigma and will always remain so. He did not believe that knowledge about him, his ideas, his beliefs, the early influence on his art, was important. 'A picture does not need translation,' he once said. 'A creative work happens. It does not need documentary evidence, dates, photographs of the artist, or what he says about his pictures. It doesn't matter who or what I am. People may think what they will of the pictures.' Yet, true as this may be of a painting here and a drawing there, when the whole body of his work is considered, to the extent this is possible, knowledge of the man and artist is bound to enrich understanding of his stylistic development and the expanding range and depth of his vision.

At the time of his visit to Devon, Yeats had spent only eight of his twenty-six years in Ireland. He was born in London only

130 JACK B. YEATS *Waiting*

four years after his father's decision to become an artist, and his early years must have been spent in the highly charged atmosphere of his father starting out in a new profession. Between the ages of eight and sixteen he was in Sligo, but in 1888 he was back at art school in London, and he did not finally settle in Ireland until about 1900. At this stage he was a mature and accomplished artist, of great range, versatility and depth of perception and understanding, and the creator of such fine drawings and watercolours as the *Pastimes of the Londoners* series, the Devonshire watercolours already referred to, the Norfolk Broads series, his circus, boxing, betting and racing drawings, and a number of those almost apocalyptic figures which were to become such an important element in his work – *The Canvas Man, The Hard Stuff, The Tinker, The Circus Clown,* *Ill. 132* *The Rake* and *Man from Arranmore.*

160

131 JACK B. YEATS *Empty Creels*

It is difficult to pin down the early influences. Mark Glaze-
brook has already pointed out the debt to Degas, although this
may well be indirect. Probably the most profound influence
came from the rich and mostly anonymous graphic illustration
which was so essential a part of journalism during the period
in which Yeats grew up, and which provided him with his first
job as an artist when he did drawings for *The Vegetarian* in 1888.
He subsequently did drawings for the *Daily Graphic* and the
Manchester Guardian, as well as a considerable amount of book
and broadsheet illustration at a slightly later stage. He learnt two
distinct things from this 'reportage': the importance of strength
and simplicity of line and composition, and the crucial importance of depicting in all these drawings 'an event'. It is fair to
say that in the greater part of all Yeats' art, drawings, watercolours, and oils of all periods, one common distinction may be

132 JACK B. YEATS
The Man from Arranmore

Ill. 133   observed: that of 'something happening'. From *Boat Race Day –*
Two Bargees Dancing an Imitation of the Sisters of the Halls through
Ills 134–5   *Riverside Long Ago* to *About to Write a Letter* and *The Two*
Travellers his work is distinguished by its emphasis upon
actions, encounters, moments of decision, moments of truth.
And if one adds to this Yeats's isolated and solitary figures, his
men of the west determined to conquer, his boxers determined
to defeat their opponents, his jockeys determined to win, his
clowns determined to captivate their audiences, then to a very
great extent the universal nature of his art may be seen in terms

162

133 JACK B. YEATS *Boat Race Day –*
Two Bargees Dancing an Imitation of the Sisters of the Halls

134 JACK B. YEATS *Riverside Long Ago*

135 JACK B. YEATS *The Two Travellers*

of the individual's encounters with the world, whether the 'world' is an opponent in a boxing ring, or 'the unknown', towards which *The Face in Shadow* is turning. And this universality is common from the early graphics, however specific their location may be, right through his watercolours, his early oils, the richly diverse range of middle period pictures, into the enigmatic landscape of his last period. The breaking down of Yeats's art into periods is only of minor importance in understanding his work. It reveals his technical development, and the points at which he reached the limits of one medium, or of one particular way of looking at his subject. But his

Ill. 137

164

136 JACK B. YEATS *Many Ferries*

imagination and his vision of life, while they grow richer, more varied and more profound, do not really change. He is a great draughtsman in *Boat Race Day*. He is a great water-colourist in *Waiting*. He is a great painter in *Empty Creels*. He is a great and wonderful artist in *About to Write a Letter*.

Ill. 133
Ills 130–1
Ill. 1

His genius tends to isolate Yeats in Irish art. *His Thoughts to Himself* describes effectively his relationship to other painters. While he worked all his mature life in Ireland, exhibiting with the RHA, the Living Art, and in one-man shows, as well as being represented in English and American exhibitions, including the famous Armory show in 1913, Yeats, both as

137 JACK B. YEATS *The Face in Shadow*

painter and person, kept himself to himself, suffered no fools gladly, took no pupils, was never seen at work, and, as already pointed out, considered that one thing only mattered about himself – the paintings which he produced. And what people thought of them was their business. 'Who the blazes is Gleizes?' he asked, when told of Evie Hone's and Mainie Jellett's work under the French cubist; and 'Ah well' was all he said when asked what advice he would give to a young artist.

Ill. 146
Ill. 145

In the Ireland to which he returned, art was shortly to be influenced by French painting through the important contribution of Evie Hone and Mainie Jellett, as well as the more conventional work of Paul Henry, who also learnt his art in Paris. Paul Henry (1877–1958) was born in Northern Ireland, studied art in Paris at Whistler's studio, and settled in Connemara almost on impulse. His landscapes reveal a superb under-

166

standing of Irish light, as in *Dawn, Killarney Bay*, and a remark- *Ill. 139*
able subtlety in his treatment of the strange and unusual
combinations of colour in his many paintings of lakes and
bogland in Connemara and Donegal. Many of these have an
extreme simplicity, just the careful composition of water and
headlands, of turf-stacks against the grey-blue hills along the
horizon, and of billowing clouds banked up above his low
horizon-line. Occasionally he could introduce figures with
great effect, as in the powerful picture, *The Turf-Carriers*, with
its echo of van Gogh. Paul Henry's wife, Grace (d. 1952), was
also an artist of considerable ability, although her landscapes are
on a more domestic scale, lacking the sense of enormous and
deserted land and sky. She also did portraits; one of her hus-
band is in the Ulster Museum. A landscape artist who worked

138 JAMES HUMBERT CRAIG *Cloud Shadows, Connemara*

139 PAUL HENRY *Dawn, Killarney Bay*

in a style quite close to that of Henry was James Humbert Craig (d. 1944). Again, he is more limited. While the technique of a painting like his *Going to Mass* in the Municipal Gallery in Cork is of a high order, the conception of the picture, the event and the landscape in which it is taking place, are rather subdued. *Tholla Bhistrie* in the same gallery is a good
Ill. 138 example of his work, while in *Cloud Shadows, Connemara* he comes close to the strong simplicity of Henry's work. George Russell (1867–1935) painted many good and simple landscapes, but was led by his highly individual imagination into a kind of fairytale world which he depicted with great charm but insufficient strength to resist an insipid quality in many of his

140 GEORGE RUSSELL ('AE') *The Potato Gatherers* .

works. At his best, as in *The Potato Gatherers*, he could display
great strength of composition and colour, and *The Gully*, in
the Municipal Gallery of Modern Art in Dublin, is a fine
example of his more typical 'soft' work. Letitia Hamilton
(1879–1964) was a landscape painter of the same period who
may be said to have combined the palette of Paul Henry with
the impressionistic style and impasto of Roderick O'Conor.
At her best her paintings are rich in colour and well composed.
Her sister, Eva H. Hamilton also painted competent landscapes
in oil. William Conor (1884–1968) conveys very well in his
oils and drawings the atmosphere in Northern Ireland, concentrating to a considerable extent on urban scenes, as in *The*

Ill. 140

Ills 109–10

141 W. J. LEECH
*Convent Garden,
Brittany*

Jaunting Car. Two watercolourists of distinction working at this time were Mildred A. Butler and Rose Barton. The former painted in a style quite close to that of Colles Watkins while Rose Barton's watercolours have a softness and individuality of colour that are all her own. She also did some book illustrations at the turn of the century.

One of the finest artists of this generation of painters is still living. W. J. Leech (b. 1881) was born and educated in Dublin and studied art at the Metropolitan School of Art under Walter

Osborne before going to Paris and the Académie Julienne. His first picture at the RHA was in 1899, and he was a full member by 1910. Even so, the freshness and simplicity of his technique places him in an influential position in Irish painting at a much later stage. His *Convent Garden, Brittany* is typical of his early experimentation with light and with a rich and thick application of paint in the manner of the *pointillistes*.

Ill. 141

Mary Swanzy (b. 1882) has a landscape style not unlike Leech's, although her technique seems generally stronger and more decisive than his, with harder colours. Maurice MacGonigal (b. 1900), the President of the RHA, is a good landscape artist, painting with rather muted colours soft, blue-grey scenes at country fairs, and occasionally quite vivid interiors. Frank McKelvey (b. 1895) is another landscape artist whose muted and soft colours suit the misty and rain-swept countryside which is generally the subject of his paintings. Charles McAuley and Maurice Wilks are two other Northern Ireland landscape artists, as well as Robertson H. Craig (b. 1916).

A group of subject and narrative painters, in style quite close to the more conventional landscape artists of the period between the First and Second World Wars, produced three figures of note: Sean Keating (b. 1889), Patrick Tuohy (1894–1930) and Charles Lamb (1893–1964). Keating, a former PRHA, is an excellent draughtsman, and his oil paintings, with their solid sense of mass and volume, have considerable strength. They evoke the romantic stoicism of the western seaboard, the rural Ireland of Synge and O'Sullivan. Charles Lamb is more diverse, tackling landscape as well as the portraits of types, like his Lough Neagh fisherman or *A Quaint Couple* in the Cork Municipal Gallery. Lamb is less florid in style, and less theatrical. Patrick Tuohy is a portrait and figure painter of great feeling whose work is seen at its best in *A Mayo Peasant Boy*. Other portrait painters working at this time were Estella Solomons (b. 1882), Sean O'Sullivan (1906–64) and Lilian M. Davidson (d. 1953). Mainie Jellett (1896–1943) and Evie Hone (1894–1955) are the great innovators in modern Irish painting. Mainie

Ills 142–4

Ill. 144

Ill. 142

Ills 145–6

142 PATRICK TUOHY
A Mayo Peasant Boy

143 SEAN KEATING
An Aran Fisherman and his Wife

144 CHARLES LAMB
A Quaint Couple

LAMB

Jellett studied art in Dublin before going to London where she worked under Walter Sickert. She then moved to André Lhote's studio in Paris, and worked there for a time on cubist theories, though modified to suit representational painting. This did not satisfy her desire to reach at least some of the fundamental truths about her art before choosing her own area of self-expression. Lhote compromised cubist theories by adapting them to landscape, and while Mainie Jellet was conscious that she might well do the same, she first wanted to explore 'the extreme forms of non-representational art'. In 1921 she and Evie Hone, with whom she had studied under Lhote, persuaded Albert Gleizes, a *cubiste intégral*, to accept them as his pupils and to teach them the fundamentals of cubist

173

theory. For ten years they alternated between periods of study in Paris with Gleizes and teaching and painting in Dublin. 'Our aim', she wrote of this period, 'was to delve deeply into the inner rhythms and constructions of natural forms to create on their pattern, to make a work of art a natural creation complete in itself like a flower or any other natural organism, based on the eternal laws of harmony, balance and ordered movement (rhythm). We sought the inner principle and not the outer appearance.'

Mainie Jellett worked out these lessons of a decade in austere abstract art of a very high order. Her dependence on form and colour led her to a profound understanding of the range and intensity of pure abstract based on the almost limitless permutation of her essentially simple material. Many of her abstracts are built up from a central 'eye' or 'heart' in arcs of colour, held up and together by the rhythm of line and shape, and given depth and intensity – a sense of abstract perspective – by the basic understanding of light and colour. It was natural for many of her abstract ideas to assume a Christian connotation, and she herself regarded as most important her 'non-representational work based on Christian religious subjects treated symbolically *Ill. 145* without realism'. Her *Deposition* is a fine example of this, her best work.

Evie Hone belonged to the same family ancestry as the other Irish artists of the same name, and was a direct descendant of Joseph Hone, a brother of Nathaniel Hone the elder. Her development and training closely followed that of Mainie Jellett. She studied under Sickert, Bernard Meninsky and also Glen Byam Shaw, before moving to Paris and working under André Lhote and Gleizes. She and Mainie Jellett held a joint exhibition in Dublin in 1924, and she continued to exhibit in group shows and on her own. But her development took her away from painting into stained glass. In spite of physical handicap, the lack of understanding of her artistic principles on *Ill. 126* the part of Sarah Purser, Evie Hone joined *An Túr Gloine* in about 1932, and with the help of Michael Healy established

174

herself as one of the leading stained glass artists of the twentieth century.

Her early training in abstract art was of value in the new medium to which she applied herself. And the fact that she moved on from Lhote to Gleizes, and the purity of form and colour, is significant. In her turn, however, Evie Hone returned in style to a severely representational art under the very strong influence of Rouault. This influence was absorbed and modified during her last and greatest period of work, and the many influences and images in her art were synthesized into some magnificent works, including the *Deposition* in the Municipal Gallery of Modern Art in Dublin, and the great Eton College *Ill. 146* window.

145 MAINIE JELLETT
Deposition

It was natural that the ideas of these two artists should have been profoundly influential in the Dublin of the 1930s, through both their work and their teaching. In 1943 Mainie Jellett founded the Irish Exhibition of Living Art, with Evie Hone, Louis le Brocquy, Norah McGuinness and Jack Hanlon among its founder members. It was born out of a justified frustration at the reactionary course pursued by the RHA and a feeling among its founder members that an annual show was needed where the paintings would matter more than the autocratic hierarchy of membership. If it re-established the plurality of groups of artists this was a necessary price to pay for the emergence of important painters, like Louis le Brocquy, whose work at that time was being rejected by the RHA.

Louis le Brocquy (b. 1916) is a singular artist with a highly *Ills 147–50* individual vision. He was largely self-taught, studying in France and Spain, and in Venice, and starting to paint in about 1939. His early work shows the influence of Manet and Degas, and is followed by a period when he was painting in a cubist style and developing themes of isolation, in terms of both tinkers (the isolation of an alien group in the community) and prisoners. This period culminated in paintings based on the theme of the family, children and of communication. The

146 EVIE HONE Chapel window, Eton College

147 LOUIS LE BROCQUY *Garlanded Goat*

148 LOUIS LE BROCQUY
Isolated Being

149 LOUIS LE BROCQUY
Caroline

paintings of this period are closely related to le Brocquy's work as a designer of tapestry, and between the late '40s and the mid-'50s he produced a number of fine works in this medium which closely parallel his oils during the same years. The *Ill. 147* influence of Lurçat is apparent in le Brocquy's *Garlanded Goat*, which is based on a painting, *Goat in Snow*, in the Leeds City Art Gallery.

During 1956 a notable change occurred in le Brocquy's style. Having reached a point of understanding with the family as the central focus, the artist returned to the even more crucial

178

problem of the existence and meaning of the individual being. From 1956 onwards, in what has been called his 'White Period', le Brocquy has been exploring the emergence of the human being as a physical and psychological form. His *Isolated Being* sums up the highly tentative nature of any artist's attempt to capture the total essence of human personality. It rejects the straightforward physical appearance of one human being as exclusive of any universal idea of humanity. In this respect it is important that le Brocquy has consistently avoided portrait painting, in spite of an early competence, and the fact that the human form has always been the basic subject of his work. A great deal of the impulse behind this approach is revealed by *Caroline*, a painting of a mongoloid child done by le Brocquy in 1956. In it the unformed and devoted face of the child, with

Ill. 148

Ill. 149

150 LOUIS LE BROCQUY *Study for Reconstructed Head of S.B.*

its mixed expression of trust and lack of comprehension, implies a fluid and flexible concept of personality, and a sense of communication which is at best very fragile and slight.

In his latest work, represented by *Study for Reconstructed Head of S.B.*, le Brocquy is applying the same restrained mixture of physical and psychological representation to public rather than private figures, in this case Samuel Beckett. Not unnaturally the dangers of such an approach are greatly increased by the

Ill. 150

180

physical familiarity of the subject, and the fact that the temptation to allow this aspect to predominate can be countered only by the extremely difficult problem of transforming psychological impressions into visual terms. The greatness of this picture lies in the way le Brocquy has captured the essence of Beckett's own complicated and obscure art in the haunted, emergent face, and the grey-flecked, whitish mist from which it seems to appear.

Patrick Scott (b. 1921) started as an architect, and his earliest *Ill. 151* paintings have a clear, strong, formal composition. He passed through a phase of very simple, almost child-like landscapes in the mid-'40s, with the elementary, horizon-line division of his

151 PATRICK SCOTT *Yellow Device*

canvases, but beyond this there is no real concern with perspective. The flat, almost diagrammatic, birds, animals and fish which form part of these early compositions are isolated from one another across the canvas in a formal pattern. In *The Sun*, painted in 1944, he made his first venture into a thematic form of composition which has been central to his art since then. The painting is of fields and sky with a massive sun low over the horizon. For the past twenty years Scott has worked mainly on this theme of extremely simple landscapes, with ever-increasing subtlety of colour, and economy of formal construction.

Norah McGuinness (b. 1903), another pupil of André Lhote, was born in Londonderry, and for some years worked in Paris, London and New York before settling in Dublin. Her landscapes are bold and strong in colour and composition, with hard, angular lines, and strong greys, browns and blues. In her latest work there is a softening of line and texture, but her most typical style is to be seen in paintings like *Morning Moon* in the *Ill. 152* Irish Arts Council collection, or *Tide Receding, Dublin Docks*.

152 NORAH MCGUINNESS *Tide Receding, Dublin Docks*

153 NANO REID *Cats in the Kitchen*

Nano Reid (b. 1910) held her first exhibition in Dublin in 1933, *Ill. 153* after studying art in that city and in Paris. From the beginning she was good at drawing, and her flexible and fluid sense of line is apparent in her oils. The colours in her paintings are muted, almost flat, and her first concern is in composition, line and movement, rather than the play of light. This takes away from her paintings some of the depth and perspective, but gives them a kind of woven texture, rich in allusion. Her subjects are domestic and immediate, and her treatment simple.

In his earlier work Gerard Dillon (b. 1916) has this same tapestry-like quality, and his many experiments with different media and varied textures indicate a dissatisfaction with the clear and lucent quality of oil paint. But his best work is direct, and his use of simple but fundamental themes, such as that connecting the clown with death, has produced some excellent

183

154 GERARD DILLON
The Brothers

Ill. 154   and powerful paintings like *The Brothers*, with its poignant and
personal statement on the theme of man's mortality. Patrick
Collins (b. 1910) has an enclosed and introverted vision, and a
sombre range of colour. His fluency in the treatment of nudes
is not matched by his landscapes, which only rarely capture the
luminous and expansive light of Sligo, Wicklow or Donegal.
But some of his nudes are fine paintings, with great softness and
strength.

Anne Yeats (b. 1919), the niece of Jack B. Yeats, is a concise
landscape and still-life artist, with an excellent sense of life, and
a growing richness of form and colour in her work. Father Jack

Hanlon (b. 1913) shows the influence of André Lhote in his colour and composition. He is an excellent watercolourist and a good painter in oils, whose simple and domestic subjects have a cleanness and brilliance of colour as well as strong composition. In *The Protestant and the Catholic Garden* his use of white betrays his first allegiance to watercolour, but the painting has strong tonal patterns and excellent balance. A strong independence of style also characterizes the work of Harry Kernoff (b. 1900), most of which concentrates on Dublin scenes and characters. Muriel Brandt is rather more formal in style, but consistently competent in portraiture, and in graphic work.

156 PATRICK HENNESSY *Imperial Rose*

Ill. 156 Two artists who have, to some degree, bridged the gap between the Living Art and the RHA are George Campbell (b. 1917) and Patrick Hennessy (b. 1915). Campbell has always been a good and active draughtsman, partly through the influence of his mother, Greta Bowen, who was an artist, and his brothers who also painted. This led to a clear and decisive linear style in his early landscapes and west of Ireland village and harbour scenes. He combined this with a good understanding of light and the use of soft greys and blues. Later he visited Spain, and the strong, hard light affected his style and use of colour. In his later work the hardness of line has been replaced by hardness of colour; this has tended to make his work rather cold, and somewhat academic in its appeal.

Patrick Hennessy is an artist with immense technical virtuosity in an age when visionaries and innovators predominate. This has obscured the highly individual nature of his work. He has a surrealist vision, and his paintings of still-life subjects, of apples and roses, of dream-like landscapes and exquisite *trompe l'œil*, have a rich substratum of meaning connected with

186

157 DEREK HILL *Tory Island from Tor More*

time, decay and death. *Imperial Rose* is an excellent example of   *Ill. 156*
the way Hennessy paints on two quite different levels.

Derek Hill (b. 1916) is an English artist settled in Ireland
whose finest landscapes belong to the wild and stormy Donegal
coast near which he lives. He has steered an uneasy course
between professional portrait painting, for which he has great
sympathy and feeling, and the more intractable material of
landscape art, for which he has greater affection. His *Tory
Island from Tor More* is a magnificent open seascape, with simple,   *Ill. 157*
controlled composition, and the brilliant, silver flash of hard
light over grey seas.

One of Derek Hill's pupils, if the term is not too inappropriate, is the Tory Island primitive, James Dixon (b. 1887).
Dixon watched Hill paint, and said he could do better. He was
given the materials, and embarked on a rich and uninterrupted
career as painter of seascapes and landscapes, mostly containing   *Ill. 158*
the events – such as the capture of muldoons, the firing of
rockets, the landing of helicopters – which break the monotony
of island life for the people off this remote north-west coast of

Ireland. But some of his paintings are merely of storms, and in their strength and colour they capture precisely the almost terrifying greyness and wildness of the islands on the Atlantic seaboard.

William Scott (b. 1913) is of Irish–Scottish parentage and was trained in Belfast before going on to the Royal Academy Schools in London. He is an abstract painter whose evolution has followed the 'inner principle' theory, after quite extensive periods as a still-life artist. His early paintings have great simplicity of composition, and reveal a great deal about his later *Ill. 159* work. *Still Life* belongs to the late '50s. He had already at that stage been painting in abstract, and had returned to the domestic still-life subjects for a period before again taking up the form

158 JAMES DIXON
Tory Island

159–60 WILLIAM SCOTT
Still Life and,
below, *Direction*

and colour compositions of the '60s. The pots and pans which make up his picture have been reduced almost to flat shapes, spaced from each other and related in terms of outline and position as well as colour.

Seen in relation to *Still Life*, Scott's *Direction*, painted some ten years later, assumes much greater abstract significance in its relationship of form and colour, and the rhythm which derives from the tensions created by this relationship.

Ills 159–60

As well as William Scott, Northern Ireland has produced a number of fine modern painters, partly as a result of the more enlightened and objective tradition of art-training established in Belfast during the late '30s and '40s. John Luke (b. 1906) was an early leader in technical innovation, and in the extreme simplification of landscape into clean line and flat, luminous colour. Lady Mabel Annesley applied modernist theories to watercolour painting and wood engraving, at which she showed considerable artistic capability. But the main figures in Northern Ireland of the '40s and '50s have been Colin Middleton, Dan O'Neill, Basil Blackshaw, and of a slightly later generation, Arthur Armstrong, T. P. Flanagan, Noreen Rice and Deborah Brown.

Ill. 161

Ills 163–5

Ills 162, 166

Ill. 161
Colin Middleton (b. 1910) has continued to experiment with style and technique throughout his development as a painter. There have been periods of surrealism, of cubist style, of extreme romanticism in which the influence of Yeats was strong, and periods when the ascetic line and form of Ben Nicholson affected his work. It has been said of Colin Middleton's notebooks that they offer 'evidence of an unsatisfied pilgrimage through the devious ways of modernism'. But if Middleton's work displays such uncertainty, and it is a justified reflection of contemporary trends in art, the reflection is conveyed in work which, in each 'period', displays great technical ability and a profound understanding of the unchanging material which forms the inspiration for his art. Perhaps his most sensitive work was done during the '40s and early '50s, to which period *The Skylark* belongs.

Dan O'Neill (b. 1920), born in Belfast, is the complete opposite of Middleton: consistent in style, constrained in his colour range, and profound in his statements on a fairly narrow area of human activity, although he is also the painter of many

Ill. 165
splendid landscapes, including *Knockalla Hills, Donegal* in the Ulster Museum, *Glendalough under Snow* in the Herbert Art Gallery in Coventry and *Clay Pit* in the Cork Municipal

Ill. 163
Gallery. *Mother and Child* is typical of his fine and original treatment of the most simple of themes.

161 COLIN MIDDLETON *The Skylark*

162 TERENCE P. FLANAGAN *On the Terrace*

163 DAN O'NEILL *Mother and Child*

164 BASIL BLACKSHAW *The Field*

165 DAN O'NEILL *Knockalla Hills, Donegal*

Terence P. Flanagan (b. 1929) has continually simplified his
concept of landscape, and his latest work in this category relies
almost entirely on the horizontal patterns of light to give depth
and perspective to his work. His earlier painting, of which *On*   *Ill. 162*
the Terrace is a good example, relied on stronger composition
with rather more subtle treatment of colour and tone.

Arthur Armstrong (b. 1924) has a very different approach to   *Ill. 166*
landscape, building up perspective in terms of line and a strong
and varied use of colour. In his oils his paint is thick, and has a
kind of pitted texture. The colours are rather muted, quite
different from the strong and varied shades in his drawings.

Basil Blackshaw (b. 1932) paints landscapes and portraits. His   *Ill. 164*
portraits have an aggressive appearance, loaded with meaning
and statement of an almost antagonistic type, which nevertheless, in their harsh honesty, have value. His landscapes are

166 ARTHUR ARMSTRONG *Rocks and Sea near Roundstone*

strong in colour and sense of space, with good light and excellent perspective.

Deborah Brown's work is almost entirely abstract, and both she and Noreen Rice frequently use collage techniques. The work of the former is pure abstract, concerned with the balance and inter-relationship of colour and form. Noreen Rice, on the other hand, is a symbolist artist, employing accepted realist subject-matter, but in a fragmented way.

Ill. 168–9 One other Northern Ireland artist of great importance is the sculptor, F. E. McWilliam (b. 1909). He was born in Banbridge, County Down, and studied in Belfast and at the Slade School in London before going to Paris. He was represented in the Herbert Art Gallery exhibition entitled 'Metamorphosis', based on the twentieth-century concern with the transfer in art from representational to abstract. This idea is central to McWilliam's work. As late as 1956 he made his completely

Ill. 168 representational *Elizabeth Frink*, yet much earlier he was experimenting with the breakdown of human form, as in *Man*

Ill. 169 *and Wife*, and in a considerable portion of his work this has been carried through into total abstract.

The tradition of sculpture in Ireland during the nineteenth century had been strong, and at the beginning of the twentieth it received new inspiration from the work of several fine sculptors in Dublin, Oliver Sheppard (1864–1941), Andrew O'Connor (1874–1941), Albert Power (1883–1945) and Jerome Connor (1876–1943). Sheppard's work has much of the turn-of-the-century, *art nouveau* inspiration in it. Albert Power's style and force are largely influenced by Rodin, and Rodin was also one of the principal formative influences on Andrew

Ill. 167 O'Connor, whose fine statue of Daniel O'Connell in the National Bank in Dame Street has been a seminal work in the development of sculpture in Ireland. Among modern sculptors

Ill. 170 the work of Oisin Kelly has a strong and vibrant quality, with many medieval echoes in the religious pieces, and a fine sense of lightness and comedy in such examples as *Teazle*. His metal *Cross* is a typical work. Seamus Murphy, the Cork sculptor

194

167 ANDREW O'CONNOR
Daniel O'Connell

169 F.E. MCWILLIAM
Man and Wife

168 F.E. MCWILLIAM
Elizabeth Frink

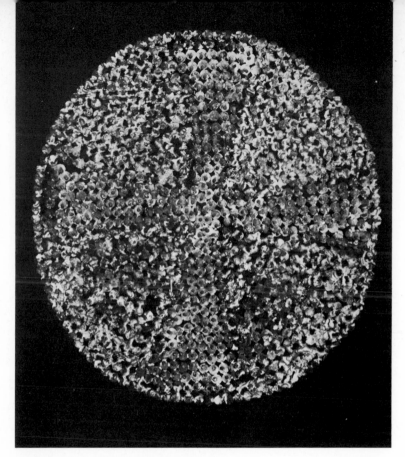

170 OISIN KELLY *Cross*

(b. 1907), has maintained a tradition of portraiture, as well as
producing religious work; and among the younger artists Ian
Stuart has established an individual style in abstract work, while
Edward Delaney has pursued the more conventional tradition
of representational sculpture.

But the two most significant sculptors are both women,
Hilary Heron (b. 1923) and Gerda Fromel (b. 1931). Much of
Hilary Heron's early work was carved in wood. It has a strength
and simplicity which derive from its return to fundamentals of
technique and expression, exemplified in her supine figure, *And
the Lord God formed Man from the Dust of the Ground*. In her work

196

171 HILARY HERON *Crazy Jane*   172 GERDA FROMEL *Tree*

she has great spatial awareness, and a tension which derives from
this. This becomes even more apparent in her relief work, some
of her carved panels, such as the *Christus Rex*, and in *Crazy Jane*.   *Ill. 171*
Gerda Fromel settled in Ireland in 1956 after studying art and
sculpture in Germany. Her work in some ways parallels that of
McWilliam, particularly in the attempt at metamorphosis of
representational concepts into abstract realizations. She uses
marble for sculptured landscapes, employing the colours and
veins and texture, but with only the most tentative presentation
of horizon and sun. Her *Tree* is a good example of her   *Ill. 172*
transitional work from realism to abstract.

197

173 THOMAS RYAN *Flight of the Earls*

Among younger painters the trends, fashions and directions in art have remained as richly diverse as they were to the painters of the '40s and '50s, who fought out the tussle between abstract and representational, between the hierarchy of academic art and the cry of the 'modern', to 'make it new!' The traditions of the Royal Hibernian Academy have been maintained by painters like Fergus O'Ryan (b. 1911); Tom Nisbit (b. 1909), a superb watercolourist; Desmond Carrick (b. 1930); Henry Healy; and two portrait painters, James le Jeune and David Hone, whose treatment of his subjects is subtle and revealing. But perhaps the most aggressive younger spokesman for the traditions of academic art in Ireland has been the Limerick painter, Thomas Ryan (b. 1929). His *Flight of the Earls* was the centre of con- *Ill. 173* troversy in the late '50s, when it symbolized the divided state of artistic loyalties in Ireland, and indicated an unreal, imagined gulf between two sorts of art. Ryan as a painter is best at land-scape. He is technically very competent, and has great sympathy for the painting of light, shadow, water and trees. Unfortunately, he believes in the artist's obligation to record his own times, and much of his energy goes into the painting of historical pictures in an outworn, strictly representational way.

Cecil King is a somewhat older painter who came late to his art, but struck out in an abstract direction with highly finished pastels and undisciplined oils. The form of his line and the soft textures of his colour have produced some excellent work in the medium of pastel. Patrick Pye (b. 1929) also works in pastel, *Ill. 174* as well as in oil and stained glass. Much of his early painting was severely muted in colour, depending on compositional form

174 PATRICK PYE *The Mocking of Christ 3*

175 ANNE MADDEN *Quadripartite Mountain Sequence, 1967 (Red)*

and balance for its effect, and mainly religious in theme. The inspiration for much of his early work came from the Italian primitives, and his understanding of colour from Mainie Jellett's work. More recently his palette has become greatly enriched, almost adding a new dimension to his work. Anne Madden (b. 1932), the wife of Louis le Brocquy, is severely abstract, although much of her inspiration comes directly from colour and tone in landscape. It is represented, however, in a highly fluid, though hard-edge, manner. She is also a sculptor. With these painters should also be mentioned Richard Kingston.

Barrie Cooke (b. 1931) settled in Ireland in the mid-'50s, in County Clare, and painted landscapes, as well as some excellent nudes and studies of birds and animals. His line is always loose and fluid, both in his drawings and in his oils, and he depends to a large extent on the subtle effects to be derived from tonal values. This applies equally to his nudes and his landscapes. His early work suited the wild and barren areas of Ireland

Ill. 145

Ill. 175

200

176 BARRY COOKE *Siobhan McKenna*

around County Clare. Subsequently he moved to Kilkenny, and the far richer landscape there struck chords of his early life in Cheshire, where he was born, and produced a series of far richer landscapes, with strong greens and yellows. His portrait and figure studies, however, have a greater richness and depth. *Ill. 176*

Michael Farrell (b. 1940) is Irish by birth only, having lived, studied art and worked in London. For his often monumental hard-edge paintings he employs Celtic motifs, although the simplified and fundamental nature of his abstract art deprives it of specific statement on the motif level, just as the balanced patterns and colours carry the abstraction beyond the severe rhythms of the artist like William Scott. *Ill. 177*

In Tim Booth (b. 1943) Ireland has one of its first good 'Pop' artists. And in the same generation of younger figures there are Tim Goulding (b. 1945), Michael Bennett, Edward Mooney (b. 1935), John Behan (b. 1938), Brett McEntagart (b. 1939), Sean McSweeney (b. 1935) and Charles Cullen (b. 1939).

177 MICHEAL FARRELL *Study I*

Ill. 178   A number of figures working in Dublin at present fit into no clear grouping of artists. Among these is Patrick Hickey (b. 1927) whose graphic work is among the best being done in Ireland, and whose paintings have grown in style and texture out of graphic processes. In his latest work these oils have included some excellent Wicklow landscapes.

Pauline Bewick (b. 1935) is a stylish and very individual graphic artist, with a particularly colourful and original treatment of animals. She is a descendant of Thomas Bewick. Her mother is also an artist in a highly individual collage technique, called by herself 'Scavenger Art'.

Finally there are two Irish landscape artists who, in their technical strength and the range of their artistic vision, exemplify the continuing resilience of this, the finest strand in the complex network of Irish art. Brian Bourke (b. 1936) is much more than a landscape painter. Indeed, some of his most

178 PATRICK HICKEY *Escarpment, Glendalough*

striking work has been done in the painting of nudes, portraits and self-portraits. But in these areas his view of life is still filled with an element of mockery and disdain. His landscapes have a far greater severity and depth. *Winter* is a composite land- scape of the artist's school grounds and building, painted partly from memory, and partly as the result of subsequent visits. In colour it is filled with the light of remembered winters, the flat, sombre mauves and blues, and of real winter, plainly observed and accurately depicted. In his foreground there are implications of wider vistas and of the arbitrary nature of choice in the painting of any scene.

Ill. 180

This aspect of Bourke's painting is exemplified in his self- portraits, which are numerous and immensely varied. They almost all have a hint of self-mockery, and many are intention- ally presenting the artist in an absurd or quite arbitrary light, such as his *Self-portrait, nude, with Fireman's Helmet.*

203

179 CAMILLE SOUTER *And So Came Spring*

Camille Souter (b. 1929) is a more restrained artist, less flamboyant in her approach, more muted in colour, and more consistently a landscape artist, although her work does also include much still-life, and periodic interest in action subjects such as circuses. Her earliest work was abstract as well as representational, and more colourful. Her later landscapes have become far more significant though restrained paintings, with excellent perspective, and with a growing element of subtlety in their conception that adds to their impact. There is great range of feeling in such pictures as *Bog – Early Morning* in the Trinity College collection, *The Last of the Radico* in the Ulster *Ill. 179* Museum, *And So Came Spring*, and *Just Before the Haymaking* in Sir Basil Goulding's collection.

180 BRIAN BOURKE *Winter*

Bibliography

The amount of writing on various aspects of Irish art is very considerable in some periods, negligible in others. No attempt is made here to cover any of the periods or special subjects exhaustively. The books and articles in periodicals listed here are those which have been consulted for the writing of this history, or are considered to be important or unique studies of their subjects.

General Works

Books

ARMSTRONG, Sir Walter. *Art in Great Britain and Ireland*. London, 1909

BELL, S.H., ROBB, Nesca A., HEWITT, J. *The Arts in Ulster*. London, 1951

BENEZIT, E. *Dictionnaire Critique et Documentaire des Peintres, Sculpteurs, Dessinateurs et Graveurs*. Grund, 1960

BRYAN, M. *Dictionary of Painters and Engravers*; first published 1816; revised G.C. Williamson, 1903–4

CAREY, William. *Some Memoirs . . . of the Fine Arts in England and Ireland*. London, 1826

GRANT, Maurice Harold. *A Dictionary of British Sculptors from 13th to 20th century*. London, 1953

GUNNIS, Rupert. *Dictionary of British Sculptors 1660–1851*. London, 1953

IRISH ART HANDBOOK. Dublin, 1943

PILKINGTON, Revd. M. *A Dictionary of Painters*. Editorial additions were made by James Barry and Fuseli, 1798, 1810

REDGRAVE, Samuel and Richard. *A Century of British Painters*. Edited by Ruthven Todd, London, 1947

STRICKLAND, Walter G. *A Descriptive Catalogue of the Pictures, Busts, and Statues in Trinity College, Dublin, and in the Provost's House*. Dublin, 1916

STRICKLAND, Walter G. *A Dictionary of Irish Artists*, 2 vols, London and Dublin, 1913

The Dictionary of National Biography

WALKER, J. Crampton. *Irish Life and Landscape*. Dublin, 1927

(WILLIAMS, John) 'PASQUIN, Anthony'. *An Authentic History of the Professors of Painting, Sculpture and Architecture who have painted in Ireland*. London, 1796

Periodicals, Catalogues, etc.

BODKIN, Thomas. *Report on the Arts in Ireland*. Government Publications Office, Dublin, 1949

ELMES, Rosalind M. *Catalogue of Irish Topographical Prints and Original Drawings (National Library of Ireland)*. Dublin, 1943

ELMES, Rosalind M. *Catalogue of Engraved Irish Portraits mainly in the Joly Collection and of Original Drawings*. Dublin, n.d.

Catalogue of Pictures and Other Works of Art in the National Gallery of Ireland and the National Portrait Gallery. Dublin, 1928

Catalogue: *Irish Houses and Landscapes*. Ulster Museum Exhibition. Belfast, 1963

Catalogue: *Pictures from Irish Houses*. Ulster Museum Exhibition. Belfast, 1961

Illustrated Catalogue: *Municipal Gallery of Modern Art*. Dublin, 1908

COSGRAVE, E. McDowell. *A Catalogue of Engravings of Dublin*. Dublin, 1905

McGREEVY, Thomas. *Fifty Years of Irish Painting*. Capuchin Annual, 1949

'The Arts in Ireland'. *Apollo Magazine*, October, 1966. (Special issue on Irish painting, furniture, etc.)

WHITE, James. 'The Visual Arts in Ireland'. *Studies*, Spring, 1955

WHITE, James and WYNNE, Michael. *Irish Stained Glass*. Dublin, 1963.

Celtic Art

DILLON, Myles, and CHADWICK, Nora. *The Celtic Realms*. London, 1967

HENRY, Françoise. *Irish Art in the Early Christian Period (to 800 AD)*. London, 1965. (The first volume of three, being the completely revised edition of the book which was first published in 1940. When completed it will be the authoritative work on Irish art during the Celtic period. Each volume will contain detailed bibliographies of the periods covered.)

JACOBSTHAL, P. *Early Celtic Art*. Oxford, 1944

Individual Artists

BARRY, James. *Series of Etchings from his Paintings in the Adelphi*. London, 1808–10

BERNARD, Bayle. *The Life of Samuel Lover, R.H.A., with Selections from his Papers*. London, 1874

BERRY-HILL, Henry and Sidney. *George Chinnery, Artist of the China Coast*. Leigh-on-Sea, 1963

BODKIN, Thomas. *Four Irish Landscape Painters*. London, 1920 (George Barret, James Arthur O'Connor, Walter Osborne, Nathaniel Hone)

BODKIN, Thomas. *Hugh Lane and His Pictures*. Dublin, 1934

CONOR, William. *The Irish Scene*. Belfast, 1944

DAFFORNE, J. *Pictures by William Mulready*. London, n.d.

DENSON, Alan. *Thomas Bodkin: a Bio-Bibliographical Survey*. Kendal, 1967

FRYER, E. *The Works of James Barry*. London, 1809

GRIGSON, Geoffrey. 'Some notes on Francis Danby'. *Cornhill Magazine*. London, 1946

LAVERY, Sir John. *The Life of a Painter*. London, 1940

LOVER, Samuel. *Legends and Stories of Ireland*. London, 1831

McGREEVY, Thomas. *Jack B. Yeats*. Dublin, 1945

MULVANEY, T.J. *Life of James Gandon*. London, 1846

O'DRISCOLL, W. Justin. *A Memoir of Daniel Maclise*. London, 1871

ROBERTS, William. *Francis Wheatley, his Life and Works*. London, 1910.

SHAW-SPARROW, Walter. *John Lavery and His Work*. London, n.d.

SHEE, Martin Archer. *Elements of Art*. London, 1805

SHEE, Martin Archer. *Rhymes on Art*. London, 1809

SHEE, Martin Archer. *Memoir*. London, 1860

STEPHENS, Frederick G. *Memorials of William Mulready, R.A.* London, 1890

YEATS, Jack B. *Life in the West of Ireland*. London, 1912

List of Illustrations

31 Maelisu: The Cross of Cong, *c.* 1123. Oak cased in copper and silver, gilt-bronze and gold decorations. National Museum of Ireland, Dublin

32 Maelisu: The Cross of Cong. Detail of the shaft. Photo Bord Fáilte Éireann

33 Mellifont Abbey. Founded 1142. Photo courtesy of the Courtauld Institute of Art, London

34 Boyle Abbey, Co. Roscommon. Founded 1146. Photo courtesy of the Courtauld Institute of Art, London

35 Cashel Cormac's Chapel, Cashel, Co. Tipperary. 12th century. Courtesy of the Courtauld Institute of Art, London

36 Jerpoint Abbey, Co. Kilkenny, carved monks in the cloisters. Late 12th century. Courtesy of the Commissioners of Public Works in Ireland

37 The Ballylongford Cross, 1479. National Museum of Ireland, Dublin

38 De Burgo-O'Malley Chalice, 1494. Silver-gilt. National Museum of Ireland, Dublin

39 God the Father, Fethard. Fifteenth century. Carved wood. National Museum of Ireland, Dublin

40 John Derrick: 'Troops on the March'. Woodcut from *The Image of Irelande*, 1581 (plate 8). Courtesy of the Trustees of the British Museum, London

41 James Gandy, 1619–89: *Portrait of Frances Molyneux, Lady O'Neil*. Oil on canvas. Malahide Castle

42 Francis Place: *View of Dublin from the Liffey Estuary*. Brush and wash, pen and Indian ink on paper. Witt Collection, Courtauld Institute of Art, London

43 Charles Jervas, 1675–1739: *Jonathan Swift*. Oil on canvas. National Portrait Gallery, London

44 Hugh Howard, 1675–1737: *Arcangelo Correlli*. Oil on canvas. Courtesy of the National Gallery of Ireland, Dublin

45 Charles Jervas, 1675–1739: *Portrait Head of Catherine Hyde, Duchess of Queensbury*. Pastel on paper. Witt Collection, Courtauld Institute of Art, London

46 Thomas Fry, 1710–62: *Portrait of an Artist*. Chalk on paper. Courtesy of the National Gallery of Ireland, Dublin

47 James Latham, 1696–1747: *George Berkeley*. Oil on canvas. By permission of the Board of Trinity College, Dublin

48 Thomas Frye, 1710–62: *Sir Thomas Wharton*. Oil on canvas. Courtesy of the National Gallery of Ireland, Dublin

49 Francis Bindon, before 1700–65: *Hugh Boulter*. Oil on canvas. Trinity College, Dublin (Provost's House Staircase). Photo courtesy of the National Gallery of Ireland, Dublin

50 Stephen Slaughter, d. 1765: *Portrait Group: A Lady and Child*. Oil on canvas. Courtesy of the National Gallery of Ireland, Dublin

51 Gabrielle Ricciardelli, *fl.* 1748–77: *Stillorgan Park and Obelisk*. Oil on canvas. Collection Mrs H.L.S. Young, Dublin. Photo Ulster Museum, Belfast

52 Anonymous: *View of Stradbally, County Leix*. Oil on canvas. Collection Major E.A.S. Cosby, Co. Leix. Photo Ulster Museum, Belfast

53 George Moore: *View of Westport House*. Oil on canvas. Collection the Earl of Altamont. Photo Bord Fáilte Éireann

54 George Barret, *c.* 1732–84: *On the Dargle*. Oil on canvas. Royal Hibernean Society

55 Francini brothers: *Marcus Curtius*, 1734. Plasterwork at Riverstown House, Glanmire, Co. Cork. Photo The Irish Georgian Society, Leixlip, Co. Kildare

56 George Barret, *c.* 1732–84: *Powerscourt Waterfall*. Oil on canvas. Courtesy of the National Gallery of Ireland, Dublin

57 James Barry, 1741–1806: *Adam and Eve*. Oil on canvas. Courtesy of the National Gallery of Ireland, Dublin

58 James Barry, 1741–1806: *King Lear Weeping over the Dead Body of Cordelia*. Oil on canvas. By permission of the Trustees of the Tate Gallery, London

59 Francis Wheatley, 1747–1801: *Nymphs Bathing, a View of the Salmon Leap at Leixlip*. Oil on canvas. From the Collection of Mr and Mrs Paul Mellon

60 Francis Wheatley, 1747–1801: *View of College Green, with a Meeting of the Volunteers, on 4th November, 1779*. Oil on canvas. Courtesy of the National Gallery of Ireland, Dublin

61 James Malton, d. 1803: *Front View of Trinity College, Dublin*. Watercolour. Courtesy of the National Gallery of Ireland, Dublin

62 Jonathan Fisher, d. 1809: *View of the Lower Lake, Killarney*. Oil on canvas. Courtesy of the National Gallery of Ireland, Dublin

63 William Ashford, 1746–1824: *The Casino at Marino, near Dublin*. Oil on canvas. Whitworth Art Gallery, Manchester

64 John James Barralet, 1747–1815: *Ruins of Ringsend Bridge, Dublin*. Sepia drawing. British Museum, Department of Prints and Drawings

65 Nathaniel Hone, 1718–81: *Self-portrait*. Oil on canvas. National Portrait Gallery, London

66 Nathaniel Hone, 1718–81: *The Piping Boy* (Camillus, son of the artist). Courtesy of the National Gallery of Ireland, Dublin

67 Horace Hone, 1755–1825: *Mrs Siddons*. Miniature. Courtesy of the National Gallery of Ireland, Dublin

68 Hugh Douglas Hamilton, 1739–1808: *Walter Hussey Burgh*. Pastel. Courtesy of the National Gallery of Ireland, Dublin

69 Hugh Douglas Hamilton, 1739–1808: *Cupid and Psyche in the Nuptial Bower*. Oil on canvas. Courtesy of the National Gallery of Ireland, Dublin

70 Thomas Hickey, 1741–1824: *An Actor between the Muses of Comedy and Tragedy*. Oil on canvas. Courtesy of the National Gallery of Ireland, Dublin

71 Jeremiah Barrett, d. 1770: *Anne Gore, Countess of Altamont*. Oil on canvas. Collection The Earl of Altamont

72 Robert Hunter, fl. 1752–1803: *Francis Hutcheson*. Oil on canvas. Courtesy of the National Gallery of Ireland, Dublin

73 Thomas Robinson, d. 1810: *The Entry of Lord Hardwick into Belfast as Lord Lieu-tenant, 27th August 1804*. Oil on canvas. Belfast Harbour Commissioners, Belfast

74 John Van Nost, d. 1787: *Thomas Prior*. Marble bust. Royal Dublin Society

75 Patrick Cunningham, d. 1774: *William Maple*. Marble bust. Royal Dublin Society

76 Edward Smyth, 1749–1812: Carved Head, representing the River Bann. Custom House, Dublin. Courtesy of the Commissioners of Public Works in Ireland

77 James Gandon, 1743–1824, architect: The Custom House, Dublin. Photo Edwin Smith

78 James Gandon, 1743–1824, architect: The Four Courts (from the Merchant's Quay), Dublin. Photo Edwin Smith

79 John Ensor, architect: Merrion Square, Dublin (1830s). Photo Edwin Smith

80 Anonymous: Waterford Glass honey jar. National Museum, Dublin

81 Anonymous: Pierced dish-cover, Dublin, 1773. Silver. National Museum, Dublin

82 James Arthur O'Connor, 1792–1841: *The Poachers*. Oil on canvas. Courtesy of the National Gallery of Ireland, Dublin

83 James Arthur O'Connor, 1792–1841: *View of Westport House*. Oil on canvas. Collection the Earl of Altamont. Photo Bord Fáilte Éireann

84 George Chinnery, 1774–1852: *Coastal Scene near Dublin*. Pencil and watercolour. Victoria and Albert Museum, London

85 William Sadler, 1782–1839: *Kings Bridge and Kilmainham Gate, Dublin*. Oil on canvas. Collection Arthur Guinness Son & Co. (Dublin) Ltd

86 Gaspare Gabrielli, fl. 1806–30: *Irish Landscape*. Gouache and watercolour. Graves Art Gallery, Sheffield

87 John Henry Campbell: *View of Dublin Bay*. Watercolour. Collection Bruce Arnold

88 Henry O'Neill, 1798–1880: *The River Blackwater near Fermoy*. Oil on canvas. Collection Michael Gorman, Dublin

89 Andrew Nicholl, 1804–86: *Mourne Mountains from the Road near Castlewellan*. Watercolour. Ulster Museum, Belfast

90 Michael Angelo Hayes, 1826–77: *Sackville Street, Dublin*. Watercolour. Courtesy of the National Gallery of Ireland, Dublin

91 Samuel Frederick Brocas, 1792–1847: *Post Office and Sackville Street, Dublin*. Watercolour. Victoria and Albert Museum, London

92 George Petrie, 1790–1866: *Gougane Barra*. Watercolour. Courtesy of the National Gallery of Ireland, Dublin

93 Nicholas J. Crowley, 1819–57: *Self-portrait*. Oil on canvas. Ulster Museum, Belfast

94 John Henry Foley, 1818–74: *Oliver Goldsmith*. Bronze. By permission of the Board of Trinity College, Dublin

95 Francis Danby, 1793–1861: *The Temple of Flora*. Watercolour. By permission of the Trustees of the Tate Gallery, London

96 Francis Danby, 1793–1861: *Liensford Lake, Norway*. Oil on canvas. Victoria and Albert Museum, London

97 Sir Martin Archer Shee, 1770–1850: *Self-portrait*. Oil on canvas. National Portrait Gallery, London

98 Richard Rothwell, 1800–68: *A Smiling Child*. Oil on canvas. Courtesy of the National Gallery of Ireland, Dublin

99 Adam Buck, 1759–1833: *'Mama don't make me beg in vain,/Pray read that pretty book again'*. Watercolour. Victoria and Albert Museum, London

100 Samuel Lover, 1797–1868: *Self-portrait*. Watercolour. Courtesy of the National Gallery of Ireland, Dublin

101 William Mulready, 1786–1863: *Self-portrait*. Pencil and oil (unfinished). National Portrait Gallery, London

102 William Mulready 1786–1863: *Bathers Surprised*. Oil on canvas. Courtesy of the National Gallery of Ireland, Dublin

103 William Mulready, 1786–1863: *The Last In*. Oil on canvas. By permission of the Trustees of the Tate Gallery, London

104 Daniel Maclise 1806–70: *A Winter Night's Tale*. Oil on canvas. Manchester City Art Galleries, Manchester

105 Daniel Maclise, 1806–70: *Portrait of Charles Dickens*. Oil on canvas. National Portrait Gallery, London

106 Daniel Maclise, 1806–70: *The Marriage of Princess Aoife and Strongbow*. Oil on canvas. Courtesy of the National Gallery of Ireland, Dublin

107 Nathaniel Hone 1831–1917: *Pastures at Malahide*. Oil on canvas. Courtesy of the National Gallery of Ireland, Dublin

108 Nathaniel Hone, 1831–1917: *Off Lowestoft*. Oil on canvas. Courtesy Municipal Gallery of Modern Art, Dublin

109 Roderick O'Conor, 1861–1940: *A Young Breton Girl*. Oil on canvas. Municipal Gallery of Modern Art, Dublin

110 Roderick O'Conor, 1861–1940: *Self-portrait*. Oil on canvas. Courtesy of the National Gallery of Ireland, Dublin

111 Roderick O'Conor, 1861–1940: *Field of Corn, Pont-Aven*. Oil on canvas. Ulster Museum, Belfast

112 Walter F. Osborne, 1859–1903: *Nathaniel Hone*. Oil on canvas. Courtesy the National Gallery of Ireland, Dublin

113 Walter F. Osborne, 1859–1903: *Hastings*. Oil on canvas. Courtesy of the National Gallery of Ireland, Dublin

114 Walter F. Osborne, 1859–1903: *Saint Patrick's Close, Dublin*. Oil on canvas. Courtesy of the National Gallery of Ireland, Dublin

115 Joseph Malachy Kavanagh, 1860–1918: *Old Convent Gate, Dinan*. Oil on canvas. Courtesy of the National Gallery of Ireland, Dublin

116 John Faulkner, fl. 1852–87: *Off Cape Clear, Co. Cork.* Watercolour. Graves Art Gallery, Sheffield

117 Edwin Hayes, 1820–1904: *Entrance to Cardiff*. Oil on canvas. National Museum of Wales

118 William Davis, 1812–73: *Junction of the Liffey and Rye, near Leixlip*. Oil on canvas. Walker Art Gallery, Liverpool

119 Sir Frederick William Burton, 1819–80: *George Eliot*. Drawing. National Portrait Gallery, London

120 Richard Doyle, 1824–83: *Design for a Fairy Tale*. Sepia drawing. Courtesy of the National Gallery of Ireland, Dublin

121 Erskine Nicol, 1825–1904: *The Emigrants*. Oil on canvas. By permission of the Trustees of the Tate Gallery, London

122 Matthew J. Lawless, 1836–64: *The Sick Call*. Oil on canvas. Courtesy of the National Gallery of Ireland, Dublin

123 William Orpen, 1878–1931: *The Model*. Watercolour. By permission of the Trustees of the Tate Gallery, London

124 William Orpen, 1878–1931: *A Bloomsbury Family*. Oil on canvas. Scottish National Gallery of Modern Art

125 Sir John Lavery, 1856–1941: *Hazel Lavery*. Oil on canvas. Courtesy of the Municipal Gallery of Modern Art, Dublin

126 Sarah Purser, 1849–1943: *Le Petit Dejeuner*. Oil on canvas. Courtesy of the National Gallery of Ireland, Dublin

127 John Butler Yeats, 1839–1922: *Jack B. Yeats as a Boy*. Oil on canvas. Courtesy of the National Gallery of Ireland, Dublin

128 John Butler Yeats, 1839–1922: *William Butler Yeats*. Oil on canvas. Courtesy of the National Gallery of Ireland, Dublin

129 John Butler Yeats, 1839–1922: *John Millington Synge*. Crayon on paper. Courtesy of the National Gallery of Ireland, Dublin

130 Jack B. Yeats, 1871–1957: *Waiting*. Watercolour. Collection Victor Waddington, London

131 Jack B. Yeats, 1871–1957: *Empty Creels*. Oil on canvas. Courtesy of the Municipal Gallery of Modern Art, Dublin

132 Jack B. Yeats, 1871–1957: *The Man from Arranmore*. Watercolour. Collection Victor Waddington, London

133 Jack B. Yeats, 1871–1957: *Boat Race Day – Two Bargees Dancing an Imitation of the Sisters of the Halls*. Indian ink on paper. Collection Victor Waddington, London

134 Jack B. Yeats, 1871–1957: *Riverside Long Ago*. Oil on canvas. Ulster Museum, Belfast

135 Jack B. Yeats, 1871–1957: *The Two Travellers*. Oil on canvas. By permission of the Trustees of the Tate Gallery, London

136 Jack B. Yeats, 1871–1957: *Many Ferries*. Oil on canvas. Courtesy of the National Gallery of Ireland, Dublin

137 Jack B. Yeats, 1871–1957: *The Face in Shadow*. Oil on canvas. Collection Victor Waddington, London

138 James Humbert Craig, d. 1944: *Cloud Shadows, Connemara*. Oil on canvas. Courtesy of the Municipal Gallery of Modern Art, Dublin

139 Paul Henry, 1877–1958: *Dawn, Killarney Bay*. Oil on canvas. Ulster Museum, Belfast

140 George Russell ('AE'), 1867–1935: *The Potato Gatherers*, Oil on canvas. Armagh County Museum

141 W.J. Leech *Convent Garden, Brittany*. Oil on canvas. Courtesy of the National Gallery of Ireland, Dublin

142 Patrick Tuohy, 1894–1930: *A Mayo Peasant Boy*. Oil on canvas. Courtesy of the Municipal Gallery of Modern Art, Dublin

143 Sean Keating, b. 1889: *An Aran Fisherman and his Wife*. Oil on canvas. Courtesy of the Municipal Gallery of Modern Art, Dublin

144 Charles Lamb, 1893–1964: *A Quaint Couple*. Oil on canvas. Cork Municipal Gallery. Photo Bord Fáilte Éireann

145 Mainie Jellett, 1896–1943: *Deposition*. Oil on canvas. Courtesy of the Municipal Gallery of Modern Art, Dublin

146 Evie Hone, 1894–1955: Chapel window, Eton College. Stained glass. Eton College, Windsor

147 Louis Le Brocquy, b. 1916: *Garlanded Goat*. Tapestry. The Dawson Gallery, Dublin

148 Louis Le Brocquy, b. 1916: *Isolated Being*. Oil on canvas. Courtesy of the Municipal Gallery of Modern Art, Dublin

149 Louis Le Brocquy, b. 1916: *Caroline*. Oil on canvas. Collection Gordon Nettleton

150 Louis Le Brocquy, b. 1916: *Study for Reconstructed Head of S.B*. Oil on canvas. Private collection, Edinburgh

151 Patrick Scott, b. 1921: *Yellow Device*. Oil on canvas. Ulster Museum, Belfast

152 Norah McGuinness, b. 1903: *Tide Receding, Dublin Docks*. Oil on canvas. Sligo County Library and Museum Art Collection. Photo Bord Fáilte Éireann

153 Nano Reid, b. 1910: *Cats in the Kitchen*. Oil on canvas. Courtesy of the Municipal Gallery of Modern Art, Dublin

154 Gerard Dillon, b. 1916: *The Brothers*. Oil on panel. The Dawson Gallery, Dublin

155 Patrick Collins: *Nude*. Oil on canvas. Collection Sir Basil Goulding, Bart., Dublin.

156 Patrick Hennessy, b. 1915: *Imperial Rose*. Oil on canvas. Ritchie Hendriks Gallery, Dublin

157 Derek Hill, b. 1916: *Tory Island from Tor More*. Oil on canvas. Ulster Museum, Belfast

158 James Dixon, b. 1887: *Tory Island*. Oil on paper. Collection Derek Hill

159 William Scott, b. 1913: *Still Life*. Oil on canvas. Ulster Museum, Belfast

160 William Scott, b. 1913: *Direction*. Oil on canvas. Collection the Arts Council, Dublin

161 Colin Middleton: *The Skylark*. Oil on board. Collection John Hewitt

162 Terence P. Flanagan, b. 1929: *On the Terrace*. Oil on hardboard. Herbert Art Gallery and Museum, Coventry

163 Dan O'Neill, b. 1920: *Mother and Child*. Oil on canvas. Ulster Museum, Belfast

164 Basil Blackshaw, b. 1932: *The Field*. Oil on canvas. Ulster Museum, Belfast

165 Dan O'Neill, b. 1920: *Knockalla Hills, Donegal*. Oil on canvas. Ulster Museum, Belfast

166 Arthur Armstrong, b. 1924: *Rocks and Sea near Roundstone*. Pastel on paper. Ritchie Hendriks Gallery, Dublin

167 Andrew O'Connor, 1874–1941: *Daniel O'Connell*. Bronze. The National Bank of Ireland, Dublin

168 F.E. MacWilliam, b. 1909: *Elizabeth Frink*. Bronze. Herbert Art Gallery and Museum, Coventry

169 F.E. McWilliam, b. 1909: *Man and Wife*. Concrete. Ulster Museum, Belfast

170 Oisin Kelly: *Cross*. Sculpture in metal. The Dawson Gallery, Dublin

171 Hilary Heron, b. 1923: *Crazy Jane*. Welded steel. Inter-continental Hotels, Dublin

172 Gerda Fromel, b. 1931: *Tree*. Bronze. The Dawson Gallery, Dublin

173 Thomas Ryan, b. 1929: *Flight of the Earls*. Oil on canvas. Collection of the Artist

174 Patrick Pye, b. 1929: *The Mocking of Christ 3*. Tempera on board. Collection Mrs Rosalinda M.F. Green, New York

175 Anne Madden, b. 1932: *Quadripartite Mountain Sequence, 1967 (Red)*. Oil on canvas. Collection The Arts Council, Dublin

176 Barry Cooke, b. 1931: *Siobhan McKenna*. Oil on canvas. Collection The Arts Council, Dublin

177 Micheal Farrel, b. 1940: *Study I, 1967*. Nylon paint on canvas. Ulster Museum, Belfast

178 Patrick Hickey, b. 1927: *Escarpment. Glendalough*. Oil on canvas. The Dawson Gallery, Dublin. Collection Mr Sean J. Hefferman

179 Camille Souter, b. 1929: *And So Came Spring*. Oil on canvas. Collection Sir Basil Goulding, Bart, Dublin

180 Brian Bourke, b. 1936: *Winter*. Oil on canvas. Munster and Leinster Bank, Ltd, Cork

Index